# ELK HUNTER
## THE SILVER BULLET ™

## Jay Houston

Published by
Jackson Creek Media Group, Inc.

# ELK HUNTER

## THE SILVER BULLET

### Jay Houston

Copyright 2017
by Jay Houston / Author

Cover photo courtesy of:
Roger Medley

Cover background courtesy
of: Kryptek Outdoor Group

Printed in the United States of America

ISBN:  978-0-9759319-4-3 (13 digit)
          0-9759319-4-6  (9 digit)

Jackson Creek Media Group, Inc.

# DEDICATED TO AUSTIN WORBINGTON

This book is dedicated to my good friend Doyle Worbington's son Austin "Worby" Worbington; an outstanding young man whose life journey though more brief than all had hoped, was nonetheless a bright and shining example to so many.

Austin was a celebrated athlete and proudly wore "2 Timothy 4:7" on his letter jacket. My heart tells me that this is how he would want to be remembered. God bless and keep you my brother. Well done good and faithful servant.

**"I have fought the good fight. I have finished the race. I have kept the faith."**

**2 Timothy 4:7**

*"When the man goes into the wilderness to change into a hunter that surviving kinship with the savage revives in his being, and all unconsciously dominates him with driving passion. Passion it is because for long he has been restrained in the public haunts of men. His real nature has been hidden. The hunting of game inhibits his thoughts. He feels only. He forgets himself. He sees the track, he hears the stealthy step, he smells the wild scent; and his blood dances with the dance of the ages. Then he is a killer, the ages roll back. Then he is a brother to the savage. Then all unconsciously he lives the chase, the fight, the death-dealing moment as they were lived by all his ancestors down through the misty past."*

*~ Zane Grey*

## CONTENTS

Jay Houston

## Why should you read this book?

In short...because it could very likely triple your chances of success from the average 8-12 percent to the 40 percent range of the most successful DIY elk hunters.

Recently I asked 25 successful individuals the following question. "If you could have 30 minutes with someone who has experienced phenomenal success, what would you ask them?" All were emphatic, they would ask about the mistakes and how he or she did it better the next time. This is the question I hope to answer for you in this book. How can you do it better the next time?

### Acknowledgements

My wonderful wife is my #1 source of encouragement. My most heartfelt love and appreciation go to my wife and soul mate Rae Ann Houston. Thanks to our daughter Ashley who provided me with the most appropriate title to the chapter *The Silver Hunter*. As always, thanks to all our children for their love and encouragement and especially to our daughter Abby who watches over us from Heaven.

As a proud Life Member of the Rocky Mountain Elk Foundation I am sold out on the premise that **Hunting Is Conservation**. As ethical elk hunters we have a responsibility to our fellow outdoorsmen and to those who will follow us to insure a lasting legacy of open lands and effectively managed game populations. If you are not a member of RMEF, I hope that you will consider joining with us. Your opinion and your voice count. Connect with RMEF at: www.rmef.org.

RMEF has remained a true and faithful partner with us for many years. I am honored that they have chosen to join with us again on this project by generously offering their endorsement. To the entire team at RMEF…thank you! Special thanks to Lisa Bishop who went the extra mile to help us develop the partnership for this book.

NOTE: A portion of every sale of this book for the first year will be contributed directly to the Rocky Mountain Elk Foundation.

For additional reading, my previous titles on this subject include:

- *Elk Hunting 101, A Pocketbook Guide to Elk Hunting*
- *Elk Hunting 201, Essentials for a Successful Hunt*
- *Elk Hunting 301, Making it Happen in Elk Country*
- *Answers for Elk Hunters*
- *Ultimate Elk Hunting: Strategies, Techniques and Methods*
- *A Hunters Field Notes (with Roger Medley)*

**Almost all of the above books are available at my website, www.elkcamp.com**

Jay Houston

## The Most Exhilarating Elk Hunt of My Life

Day five of my New Mexico hunt went down in my elk hunting history as the craziest yet most glorious day of elk hunting in my life. Bulls were screaming and bugling from every point of the compass. Bulls to the

Jay Houston

left, bulls to the right...which direction should I go?  They were so close; I had to ditch my boots to remain undetected.

Bowhunting bull elk in northern New Mexico can be, if conditions are right, the pinnacle of the elk hunting game. The quantity of available bulls is excellent and the opportunity to arrow a 300-class Pope and Young bruiser is very possible.  The elevation ranges from 3000-4500 feet on average making for a far less physically challenging hunt than those found at higher elevations in my home state of Colorado.  I was hunting a private ranch by invitation of my long-time friend, outfitter and fellow elk hunter Bill Glisson. Bill owns **The Timbers at Chama** and manages about 10,000 acres of prime elk habitat for his outfitting operation.

The terrain around the Brazos Peak area of northern New Mexico is a mixture of vast aromatic sage flats interspersed with random fingers of Piñon-juniper (PJ) and other dark timber. Unlike elk country farther north, the challenge for bowhunters in northern New Mexico is the lack of cover from which to plan an effective stalk on elk, which are often found feeding out in the sage. On this particular hunt, our plan was to spend mornings and mid-day glassing from the cover of the Piñon-juniper while trying to locate and cow-call nearby bulls to our hidey hole.

The flats, that seemed to go on for miles, were also home to a truly healthy population of muleys who served as the local security system for all the critters nearby. One misstep and a dozen sets of ears would instantly turn towards the offender effectively alarming, the other muleys and the elk. Mule deer by their nature are curious critters which doesn't always work in the elk hunter's favor. More than a few times we found ourselves pinned down by one or more of the overly inquisitive

9

Jay Houston

and ever alert muley does. Throughout the course of our hunt we managed to encounter a couple of really nice bucks that I believe would have scored well into the 180-190 class. We could have put a stalk on them but since mule deer season was still months away, and I didn't have a deer tag, these bucks were off the table for me on this hunt. Though they did keep me drooling and on always on my toes. Late afternoons were usually spent in or near the fringes of dark timber set up on small tanks (watering holes) that the elk were frequenting.

For those unfamiliar with the licensing process, elk tags in New Mexico are only available via one of two avenues: the state wide lottery (draw) or the acquisition of a land owner voucher which allow the hunter to purchase a tag from the state without having to be successful in the draw. Land owner (LO) vouchers almost always come with a high price tag as they have become a profit center for ranch management. Prices can range from $500 per voucher to as high as $7500 per voucher depending upon the part of the state that the voucher is good for. Units in and around the renowned Gila National Forest in western New Mexico demand some of the highest prices. Hunting the "Gila" offers some of the only public land hunting opportunity in the country for bulls in the lofty 400 plus B&C range. If you are paying for a guided hunt, vouchers are the preferred method for insuring that you are going to get a tag, but they can add significantly to the price of the hunt itself. Some guided hunt prices include the LO tag. Be sure to ask any outfitter that you contact if their hunt price includes the LO tag. Keep in mind that there is a very limited supply for any given area and they can disappear quickly. When you find a hunt that looks good and includes an LO tag, I suggest you jump on it.

**Elk Hunter Tip: For highly sought after elk hunting opportunities, the adage...*you snooze you lose* is the rule not the exception.**

10

Jay Houston

## ELK HUNTER...The Silver Bullet

Day one of our elk hunt found our gaggle of hunters, guides and camera guys (they prefer to be called videographers) heading out well before sunrise hiking to the top of a nearby mesa on the main ranch. As we began the ascent, I casually switched on my red lens headlamp as I had many times prior to keep from face planting myself into rocks or cactus which was everywhere. In short order the guide behind me taps me on the shoulder and suggests that I turn it off. My experience was that it would have no adverse effect on the game so I asked why. He suggested that I just allow my night vision to adjust for a few minutes, and I would soon be able to see my way in the darkness just fine. He was right! In just a matter of a couple of minutes my vision had adjusted and I was able to make my way up the trail without any problem.

My hunting partner and good friend Lance Schul and I set up on opposite ends of the mesa hoping to ambush elk coming up from the river below where they fed throughout the night. After about two hours of gentle cow calling, neither of us saw or heard elk, so we determined that we arrived too late. The elk had already crossed the mesa ahead of us heading to their bedding areas in the dark timber. We made a plan to adjust our alarm clocks the following morning to get us in place ahead of the elk, and hoped for a better opportunity to score on a New Mexico wapiti.

After a quick powwow, we all decided to drop down off the mesa and try our hand in some of the patches of dark timber nearer the ranch. That plan failed to produce an opportunity as well, so we loaded up our gear and headed back to the lodge for something to eat. I want to give a real shout out to the cooks at The Timbers. Every meal featured the best examples of local cuisine and was prepared with the same care as if they were cooking for their own family.

Jay Houston

Following a filling lunch, mid afternoon on day one found Bill, Lance and I working through options for the evening hunt. Knowing that the elk would soon be making their way back across the top of the mesa that evening on their way down to the river, we crafted a plan that we hoped would result in elk backstraps for dinner. Just a quick note, Bill only hires local guides for his outfitting business. His guys are top notch and know the land well, having grown up in the area. Some outfitters choose to hire guides who actually live 1000 miles away. So it pays to do your homework if you are planning and paying for a guided elk hunt. (Let us help. Find us at **www.huntconnections.com**)

The late afternoon found our gaggle headed out on foot slowly making our way back towards the mesa. Working our way through one small patch of PJ after another we began to hear tale tell sounds of elk walking over rocks ahead of us. Our guide indicated that there was a dry creek bed a few hundred yards ahead and that elk were likely working their way across the rocks as they moved back towards the mesa. Since the sound seemed to be coming from one direction, Lance and I decided to split up and try to cut them off from opposite sides.

As I reached the dry stream bed, I realized I was going to make as much noise or more than the elk had by walking over the rocks, so I quickly removed my boots (which would become a daily occurrence) and starting creeping across the rocks and up the lower slopes of the mesa in my socks hoping to catch up with the elk heading to the river.

I had not gone very far when I caught sight of two cow elk standing atop the ridge directly in front of me at about 200 yards. Regrettably, they had me dead to rights. I froze. To make matters worse, a respectable bull silently appeared in front of me walking in their direction offering no shot. He had no idea that one so determined to deliver his demise

12

was stalking just 75 yards behind him. Fully aware that those two cows were laser sighted on me, I nevertheless still tried to catch up to the bull without letting him know I was behind him. I was creeping from one PJ bush to another trying to keep at least one bush between me and the bull at all times. This game of cat and mouse went on for almost 20 minutes as the bull was in no hurry. He would take a few steps. I would take a few. Thinking back, perhaps I should have taken bigger steps. My heart was pounding as I expected the cows to bark at any second, but the angels were smiling on me and the cows never did. Eventually the bull may have sensed something as he quickened his pace and began to open the distance between us, leaving me in his dust. I was frustrated, but also elated at having successfully tracked and trailed this bull for almost half an hour and he never knew I was back there. I felt like the Captain of the Los Angeles class attack sub, USS Dallas, in the film *Hunt for Red October;* silently stalking the Russian ballistic missile submarine.

As the bull crested the ridge far out of bow range, he turned perfectly broadside showing off his 320 or so rack as a possible tribute to my stealthy efforts before dropping over the back of the ridgeline for the river below. Day one ended, score: Elk 2, Hunters 0.

Unfortunately days two and three were repeats of day one with us always a step behind the elk. No matter how early we got out, the elk always seemed to have passed our position before we arrived. Mid days were spent cruising interior roads with one of our guides in a pickup. I felt that this was useless, but he kept swearing that it worked for him all the time. I think it did *'work for him'* because didn't have to get out and walk. It just didn't work for us.

On day four I decided to focus my hunt on the 400 acre main ranch while Lance tried his luck on one of Bill's leased properties. I still hunted throughout the morning and early afternoon with no luck. Even though we were hunting very close to the rut in mid September, the air was totally void of any elk talk. No cows chirping, no bulls bugling...nada.

As the sun began its decent, I decided to relocate and set up near one of the water holes on the back side of the ranch hoping for some evening action. Bill had setup a ground blind that had a great view of the water hole; but it gave no view of the opposite hillside due to the way it was situated. After 30 minutes I began to hear elk talk coming down the hillside, which I could not see. So I quietly exited the blind and backed myself into a small patch of PJ. As I scanned the hillside, a line of cows and calves began to drift out of the timber coming down the hill. Hoping for a bull to follow I stayed put. After 10 minutes, I heard a sound over my left shoulder. Slowly I moved my eyeballs in that direction to discover a small elk calf standing about ten feet from me. It was starring right at me. Every few seconds it would jump one direction then another as if it was playing a game, but never did its eyes leave mine. After a few minutes it actually became fun watching the antics of this youngster that was oblivious to any potential threat than I might pose. Abruptly the youngster stopped jumping and froze. Suddenly the loudest, most piercing, elk alarm bark that I have ever experienced, shot out of the calf's momma's throat. She was standing no more than 15 feet from me. She had appeared without a sound. How long she had been standing there I do not know. I turned, she starred. We both locked eyes waiting for what would happen next. I knew then that the youngster was hers, and I was not really comfortable being between the two of them. Fortunately, momma chose to exercise the *better part of valor* and just turned and walked off with the youngster on her tail. I did not kill an elk that day, and fortunately an elk did not kill me. It was a great day to be an elk hunter.

Jay Houston

O' dark thirty the next morning, found me deep in the dark timber with one of Bill's younger guides. As we hunkered in some old growth pine, the bulls were already bugling....EVERYWHERE! The rut switch had been thrown ...the game was on. There were bulls bugling in every direction. Seriously! Near bulls, far bulls, big raspy bulls and lesser bulls. It was like listening to an orchestra tuning up in the pit before a performance. There was elk sound everywhere. Four days of famine...now elk chaos. I was experiencing elk hunting at its best.

We did not know which way to go first. So we just decided to sit tight and see what would happen. Pretty soon the elk made our minds up for us as my newbie guide starts up with his cow call. Immediately he gets a response, and I visually pick up a respectable bull coming right at me from about 80 yards out. The cow calling guide had placed himself directly behind me, and the bull was going to trample me to get to the cow he was hearing. Knowing that I was going to have no shot head on, I quickly repositioned myself about 15 yards offset in the hope that the bull would not detect my move and pass by giving me a shot. Seeing me move, the guide thinks something is wrong and he too repositions 15 yards... again right behind me. Argh.... This time the bull caught the guide's movement and blew out of there, but the "game" was far from over.

For the next two hours it was like *The Charge of the Light Brigade*, bugles to the left of them, bugles to the right, into the valley of death...... bull elk were bugling everywhere. I found myself in rocks again, so off came my boots (took me hours to find them again) as two bulls bugled close by to my left. I was unable to see them due to the nearly solid brush. They began pulling away, and after four or five minutes of trying to close the distance, I knew I could not catch them.

15

Jay Houston

No problem, two more were bugling at what I guessed to be 60 yards to my right, but again I could not catch a glimpse due to the dense brush.

As I was silently moving through another patch of dense undergrowth, I caught a momentary movement of dark gray in the thick brush immediately to my front, a mere five yards away. I could not see anything that resembled an elk, but I could hear the elk breathing. As quiet as a ghost, I slowly dropped down onto my knees to look beneath the brush to see if I could see any better. Not two yards from me I spy a bull lying in some pine straw at what I guessed was six feet! But there was still no shot, only gray mud caked hide and an antler tip. I could not even tell which way he was lying. Two yards!!! No shot. I tried to figure a way to draw my bow sideways parallel to the ground about six inches above the dirt. I could not do it.  This was insane. My adrenaline was through the roof. My heart rate was off the chart.

As quickly as it had begun, the ruckus settled down and the dark timber returned to its normal stoic silence. What happened that wonderful morning I have no idea. Where did they disappear to? Again...no idea. I had never experienced anything like that morning before, and have not since...but it was glorious.

That afternoon, I had my final encounter of our hunt. While this tale has been shared in another book, the previous part of the story is shared here for the first time. The hunt we were on was being filmed for a major outdoor TV show. David Drew, our camera guy and I were out working through the timber when we came upon a well used elk trail with elk coming up it. I could see three cows about 100 yards down the trail which was somewhat downhill and I could hear a bull glunking behind them. Quickly I disappeared behind the only nearby tree and David dropped down to become a rock. As the lead cow approached I knew I would have to draw with her still at 60 yards because there was open ground between us the rest of the way. So I draw and do my best imitation of a tree waiting on the bull to show himself. I don't know exactly how long I was at full draw, maybe a minute, but eventually the bow won and I had to let down. The cows saw my movement and bailed off the side of the trail to my left. There was no shot as my bow was on the right side of the tree. I spied the small 5x5 bull bailing off the trail behind his cows.

Literally, less than a minute after the small bull and his cows bailed off the trial, I detect movement at my one o'clock position. I cannot believe it, but an even more impressive bull is weaving a respectable set of antlers through the Gambol Oak brush at no more than 50 yards. Again, the brush is really thick and I'm looking for a shooting lane as I draw my bow on a second bull in less than two minutes. Quickly, I glance over my shoulder to confirm that the camera guy is ready. He says, "I'm on him, any time you are ready."  As I turn back to the bull, I see this small 6-inch diameter hole in the brush about 40 yards out and start willing...praying for this bull to walk behind that clear 6-inch hole as I center my pin. He does...can you believe it...the bull walks into the only clear lane available as I touch off the shot. Whack...the bull spins and heads back up the hill. After five arduous days I've finally closed the deal on a New Mexico bull. We high-five one another while giving the bull some time to expire. After a less than appropriate wait we begin our trek to the last spot we saw the bull.

I am looking for blood, or any sign to confirm what I already know, when I hear David say "Jay...check this out." I walk over expecting the blood that I knew must be there to see him pointing his finger at my arrow, stuck solidly in the 1" gambol oak branch that had been at the top of the 6" shot zone. My emotions were just like they say...Ecstasy to Agony.

Once I got over the shock I had to laugh...to keep from crying. I asked him if he got the shot on tape hoping that somehow my honor would remain intact with no video tape. "You bet" he says...."got every bit of it." Never fails, if I am going to mess up in the elk woods, there will always be a skilled videographer there to get it all on tape. It was an amazing yet crazy elk hunt that I will never forget. All's well that ends well. I was fortunate to be invited to return to the ranch two years later, and harvest a nice bull that is hanging on my wall as I pen this story for you.

*"In any moment of decision, the best thing you can do is the right thing, the next best thing is the wrong thing and the worst thing you can do is nothing."* ~Theodore Roosevelt

## The Silver Bullet

In folklore, a bullet cast from silver often is portrayed as the only weapon that is effective against supernatural antagonists. Essentially, the silver bullet was perceived as a single mystical solution to a monstrous problem. Since those early times, this mythical concept of a silver bullet has morphed into our 21$^{st}$ century perception of a singular strategy, tactic, or application that would result in a solution to all of our problems with minimal investment or effort.

In the spirit of transparency I share with you that I have more than a little silver in my hair. Most of this silver is the result of the long days, knee busting, thigh burning miles, countless frustrations, and even a few victories that I have experienced as an elk hunter of 20 plus years. My goal in writing this book is to share this acquired "silver" to help you become a more successful elk hunter, to help you hunt smarter.

Successful elk hunters are an extraordinary breed of folks who prepare themselves physically and mentally year-round.  Whether hunting agonizingly long days in razor thin air above timberline, or navigating dark timber jam-packed with chest high deadfalls that can snap a leg without warning, or hanging on for dear life to a bat-crazy mule while she tries to use you as a stepping stone to get out of a bog, But elk

19

Jay Houston

hunters are no different than the rest of our brethren who take to wild places each fall. **If there is an easier way out, i.e. a silver bullet, we are always looking for it.**

When internalized, information or data becomes knowledge. **And knowledge is far and away the most lethal weapon you can acquire.** If you can hang on for the ride, you will discover critical knowledge required to enable and equip you to become a much more successful elk hunter.

What I refer to as the Silver Bullet has three parts. No single part produces results on its own, but when combined they form a highly effective solution that will serve you for a lifetime.

**KNOWLEDGE + EFFORT+ PERSERVERENCE (GRIT) =**

**THE ELK HUNTER'S SILVER BULLET**

Corey Jacobsen, a nine time world elk calling champion, lifelong elk hunter and owner of Elk101.com surveyed nearly 10,000 elk hunters. The purpose of the survey was to better understand specifically what those surveyed believe contributed to their success. The nugget that I found most compelling in Jacobsen's survey analysis was the result that those hunters who had spent the most time in pursuit of knowledge had the highest elk hunting success by far. Success rates in the group that sought knowledge at every opportunity was in the 40 percent range, more than three times the overall elk hunting success average of 12 percent.  Rightly, Corey concludes **that the more successful hunters "have a desire to learn and a desire to get better."**

I have successfully hunted elk for over 25 years, having hunted with many even more skilled elk hunters from which I learned. I have traveled the country from Colorado to Oregon, Arizona to Idaho and more recently from Kentucky to Pennsylvania gathering generations of elk hunting wisdom. The sum total is now included in this single information resource for every elk hunter. If you want to become a consistently successful elk hunter you have to persevere, and you have to hunt smart. It is the later component that is the subject of this book.

Recently, I was watching an episode on one of the hunting channels where the viewers witnessed an inexperienced archery elk hunter pass up slam dunk shots on not one but two HUGE bulls. They were both inside of 25 yards, with multiple clear shot opportunities. I wanted to crawl into the TV to find out what this hunter was thinking. I observed this guy who, to my surprise, stated that he had never seen a bull elk up close, much less killed one because, as he shared, "it was the first day of his hunt and he didn't want it to end so quickly." Argh......! Folks please, please hear me on this. If you have never before killed an elk and you have the opportunity to harvest a legal animal be it a bull or a cow....TAKE THE SHOT! Any shot opportunity is statistically a 1:8 chance, meaning only one in every eight hunters has such an opportunity.

On my second ever mule deer hunt in southern New Mexico. I made the same unwise decision, which I have regretted ever since. I can still vividly picture that 4x4 muley buck in my sights. He was the only shot opportunity I was offered throughout the hunt...but it was the first day. Perhaps this is why when I saw this hunter pass on two monster bulls; I was, to say the least, a bit troubled. If you have not heard this before, memorize this....take it to heart...Never pass up a bull (or a buck) on day one of your hunt that you would be happy to put in the cooler on the last day. Never! Hunt smart. So how do you put yourself into such a position to kill a nice bull?

Jay Houston

## Plan, Position, Persevere

**Make a Plan...Execute the Plan**
Though most would not admit it publically, thousands of elk hunters spend their limited elk hunting days wandering the high country without direction hoping to get into some elk. A good friend, who lives in great elk country shared with me some years ago that his early elk hunting was more like taking his gun for a walk. Since that time, Larry has gotten smart on elk, refined his plan and consequently, he gets into the elk on a regular basis. Folks, wandering the high country is not a plan for killing elk. I'm sure that you have at some point in your life heard the following acrostic, *Prior Planning Prevents Poor Performance.*

A simple hunt plan assumes that you have done your homework and identified one or more areas that over time hold good quantities of elk and contain the age class of bulls that you are interested in. Most states offering elk hunting provide herd dispersion statistics that are available to you at no charge via their online portals. If you are still unable to identify areas that hold good quantities of elk, email me at jay@HuntConnections.com.
So what does a basic plan for success look like? This is not rocket science.

Jay Houston

**Step 1**

Identify quality food sources, water sources, bedding areas and the times that the elk in your area are using each of these. While some amount of scouting online using tools like Google Earth can help narrow your search for food and water sources; locating bedding areas and determining times of use and lanes of access can only be determined by boots on the ground scouting. This means you need to <u>plan at least one pre-season scouting trip</u> to gather this information. If an extra trip is not in the cards, then take copious notes about these key items while you are hunting so that you can review them post season and use this information to update and improve your battle plan for the following season. <u>Food, water and security are the top three needs</u> on every elk's checklist. Finding these and discovering the routes that the elk are using to move in and out of these areas will greatly increase your chances of success. This is a lot of work. It includes mile upon mile of humping up ridges and down into holes (valleys) and basins, but this is the level of effort that every successful elk hunter commits to. I want to encourage you to make this level of commitment. This is step one in your plan to increase your chances of success from the average 12 percent to the 40 percent level of the most successful elk hunters.

Albert Einstein defined insanity as *"doing the same thing over and over expecting different results."* Let's all take a tip from one of the smartest men in history and not repeat those efforts that failed to put elk in the freezer in years past. Hunt smart and make sure that you take enough time to build a proper plan.

23

Jay Houston

## Step 2

Once you have identified these three key areas you need to determine where to best locate your base camp so that you can access these areas. Your camp should be far enough from feeding and bedding areas that your camp routines and odors do not penetrate those areas you plan to hunt. Generally, I locate my camp a **minimum** of two miles away if I plan to cook in camp. If you are spike camping with a cold camp (no cooking or fires) you may be able to cut this distance down a little but not much.

## Step 3

Determine exactly how long it will take you to navigate your way to your morning stand site...in the dark. This is something many hunters fail to take into account...so they just guess. I too have been guilty of this as I shared earlier in my story of elk hunting in New Mexico and arriving late to my stand only to discover that the elk had already passed by. Learn from my mistake and know how long it will take you to get to and from your stand....quietly.

## Step 4

Once you have reached your stand site, identify every available shooting lane taking care to use your rangefinder to determine the distance to easily identifiable landmarks within each lane. If I am hunting open country, I may have two or three known ranges for each lane. If you are hunting dark timber, one landmark may be sufficient. Given that wind changes I usually ID more than one stand in a given area so that I have options if the wind is bad from a particular stand on a given day. Hunting with the wind at your back is a waste of time. Make a plan that gives you options.

Jay Houston

**Positioning Is Critical**

If you want to catch fish, sooner or later you will have to get in the water.

Positioning is the place you occupy in the field of elk hunters in relationship to other hunters. Whether in life, business, or in elk hunting...success is fundamentally reliant upon superior positioning. We have to ensure that we place ourselves in the best position to achieve our goals relative to the competition. Winning consistently at elk hunting requires positioning yourself in the top five percent of all elk hunters.

Chase Elliott, driver of the Hendrick Motorsports #24 car and a rising star in NASCAR's Sprint Cup Series might have been just another kid who liked to drive fast were it not for the positioning, encouragement and tutelage of his father and former NASCAR great Bill Elliott. A high school senior with a blazing 90 MPH fast ball is just another 18 year old jock unless he or someone acting on his behalf puts him in front of a MLB scout with radar. So how is positioning relevant to becoming a more successful elk hunter? Let's quickly break it down.

- **Knowledge position** - you know more about elk and how they use their environment than most elk hunters.
- **Skill Set position** - you are more proficient with your weapon of choice than most elk hunters. You are an expert.
- **Geographical position** - you know where the elk feed and bed and the routes they use to transit between these areas and you have the ability to put yourself there in a timely manner.
- **Grit position** - you must be willing to stick with it, to make whatever effort is required to put yourself in position for a shot.

25

**Perseverance is the #1 Key to Successful Elk Hunting**

*Perseverance is defined as: (1) the steady persistence in a course of action, a purpose, especially in spite of difficulties, obstacles, or discouragement; (2) the quality that allows someone to continue trying to do something even though it is difficult; (3) continued effort to do or achieve something [like elk hunting] despite difficulties, failure, or opposition.* ~Merriam-Webster

In the language of the elk hunter, perseverance means that you are committed to doing whatever it takes: i.e., going as far as required, sitting silently for hours in cold or even snow, circling three miles around a mountain to get the wind in your favor when a straight line stalk is less than a mile.

You are committed to climbing out of your warm sleeping bag at 2 AM when you are awakened by a bugling bull, and heading out in the freezing cold darkness, so that you can close the distance on that single bull if he goes silent just before sunrise.

In my prior life I flew fighters for the Air National Guard. From time to time I was privileged to represent the Guard at air shows across America. In addition to the aerial display we would put on, which was really fun to do, we also provided static displays where we would stand beside the jet and answer questions from those attending. Invariably, there would always be at least one young person who would ask the question, "What do I have to do to fly one of those?" My answer was always the same. You have to decide just how badly you want it. The training is long and can seem brutal at times. The impact on your social life can be painful. The amount of effort that you will have to commit to is probably far beyond anything you have ever attempted. But in the

26

Jay Houston

end, you too can become a fighter pilot if you are willing to commit and persevere.

**Elk Hunter Tip:** *Your success in this endeavor, should you choose, will be largely determined by your level of commitment, determination and perseverance... essentially GRIT.*

Grit sometimes referred to as tenacity can make all the difference in the outcome of your hunt. To make my point about grit, briefly consider General George Patton.

### General George Patton's Secret to Success: GRIT!

History is an amalgam of view points, perceptions and remembrances. In the case of General George S. Patton history [and cinema] portrays him as, among other things, a military mastermind and a brilliant tactician. In fact however, biographers generally agree that General Patton was anything but intellectually brilliant. He actually battled with dyslexia his entire life. What made Patton a success in so many of his endeavors was his tenacity or grit. Where many might have just given up, Patton purposed that he would make whatever effort was necessary to ensure his success. Many concur that it was his relentless grit that was such a determining factor in his many achievements.

It is this level of commitment and perseverance, this grit, which I believe makes the difference between successful elk hunters and those who "just take their gun for a walk in the woods."

### Becoming a Successful Elk Hunter
I am not going back to basics in this book. My *Elk Hunting 101-301* series is a great resource to revisit the fundamentals. Look for them on our

website at **www.elkcamp.com** or on Amazon.com. We are going to talk about principles that each of us have to get our head around if we are to have any hope of succeeding at this great adventure called elk hunting. Your elk hunt is 100% what you make of it. You are responsible.

When I was 14 years old I was sitting in a tent with three or four other guys getting ready to chow down on a sack lunch that I had brought along for the first night of our camping trip since we would not be cooking by the fire. As I looked around the tent for my "dinner" it was nowhere to be found. I started getting really hungry and a bit on low blood sugar, so I start asking the guys if they have seen my brown bag. None of them seemed to care. So I start turning the tent upside down looking for FOOD! Not finding anything, I begin turning the guys upside down. They were not too happy about this and it started to get a bit rowdy in the small tent. When I upended # 3, Chris, I discovered my long lost dinner parked under him smashed flat and smelling like...well Chris. Now angry and even lower blood sugar combined to drive me into some kind of frenzy all over Chris. Somehow a rather loud expletive slipped out and it wasn't long before Jack, one of the adults in our group stuck his head in the tent asking "who said that?" Trying to duck responsibility, I pointed out the back of the tent and said that the culprit went out the back. I didn't want to get in trouble. I did not want to accept the responsibility for my actions. Jack grabbed me and snatched my 14 year old backside right out of that tent and gave me a serious heart to heart about being responsible for my own actions. I never forgot that evening or that lesson, and since that night I have made a point to assume the responsibility for my own life and decisions, not leaning on others or blaming others. Flash forward: **Lesson learned...individually each of us is responsible for our elk hunt.**

28

## Getting Your Head in the Game &
## Your Check Book in Order

For 34 years when I wasn't hunting, I occasionally played golf. While I had the physical ability and understood the rules and mechanics of golf, my game never rose above the level of a mediocre player. I spent hours and hours on the links. I purchased more expensive clubs. Then I purchased even more expensive clubs...all to no avail. Not long after my 50th birthday, my frustration with the game won out, and I made a co-

29

worker the greatest golfing deal of his life by selling him my clubs...cheap. I took them out of the back of my car, put them in the trunk of his and walked away...never looking back.

Some three years later during a chance conversation with a very good golfer the light bulb came on as to why my game had never matured. I learned that golf (like so many other endeavors such as elk hunting) is really a head game. There is of course the physical aspect, but more than anything becoming a successful golfer, like becoming a successful elk hunter, requires us to get our head in the game. The following is fundamental to becoming a consistently successful elk hunter. If you are serious about killing elk, you have to get your head into the game.

## Mental Discipline
Discipline and judgment are two key personal attributes that distinguish responsible adult behavior from that of a child or adolescent. Discipline often refers to our training. Discipline is when you use reason to determine the best course of action regardless of your desires, which may be the opposite of fun. Judgment refers to how we as individuals choose to incorporate discipline into our lives.

**Elk Hunter Tip:** *For the elk hunter mental discipline can make the difference between success and failure of your hunt.*

Statistically, 80% of all elk hunters hunt within one mile of some sort of road. Years of collective elk hunting experience confirm that the majority of elk live more than a mile from any road in order to avoid human contact. Folks, in this regard elk just like us are not stupid. If we go somewhere and someone starts shooting at us...we go somewhere else to avoid the fireworks. Discipline compels us to then push ourselves beyond that one mile threshold and when necessary even further.

This mental discipline has to begin right now. It's really not hard at all. You have already made thousands of decisions in your life that affect the outcome of future events. You purpose to keep enough money in the bank account so your checks don't bounce. You plan to fill up the gas tank so that you don't run out of gas. You know better than to argue with your wife because ...well it's just not a smart thing to do. Each of these decisions requires that you engage some measure of mental discipline.

In the case of your next elk hunt you also need to make certain decisions right now that will affect the outcome of that future hunt. When we fail to engage discipline, we are setting ourselves up for possible failure. We are leaving ourselves open to our whims of the moment, adverse environmental conditions, challenging terrain, or fatigue.  The smartest elk hunter makes their decision about how they will handle adversity in the field long before they encounter it. The smartest elk hunter commits to all the tasks involved in a successful elk hunt long before they leave home. If we wait until we are in the field to decide how we are going to deal with the challenges of each days hunt, we are not planning to succeed. We are surrendering our long waited and expensive elk hunt to serendipity, fate or chance.  Consistently successful elk hunters leave as little as possible to chance. Make a plan. Execute the plan. Hunt the plan.

**Your Physical Ability is Critical**
On average I speak with a few hundred elk hunters every year helping them plan their upcoming hunt. We discuss just about every aspect of their desired hunt from the preparation, to the finances, to the actual hunt itself. We discuss strategy, gear, calling...absolutely every aspect including preparing themselves physically for the rigors of their

31

upcoming hunt. If the hunter has already spent time hunting the high country, this part of the conversation is rather short. For those who are first timers or perhaps elk hunted lower elevations in Washington or Oregon, I cannot over emphasize the importance of preparing themselves physically for elk hunting at higher elevations. If feedback is any measure, a fair percentage of these new elk hunters do not pay attention to this part of my advice, and almost every time they call and tell me after the hunt that they wished that they had listened to my advice about their physical preparation. For the unprepared, hunting higher elevations will kick your backside. Truthfully, in over 20 years of talking with elk hunters, not a single person [Ever] has said anything resembling 'that was an easy hunt.' Take a lesson from a US Navy SEALS saying: *"The only easy day was yesterday."*

Let's look at a couple of real world examples of what I am talking about:

 I'll call hunter guy #1 George. George was a successful businessman from a large city back east who met me at an RMEF (Rocky Mountain Elk Foundation) banquet. He said he was an experienced eastern big game hunter and would like for me to book his elk hunt for the following year. I said great, I'm ready to help and my help is going to start right now. The gentleman was obese. I told him he needed to lose some serious weight before his hunt. I was very concerned that the strenuous daily regimen of an elk hunt combined with thin air at altitude might end his life. I suggested that at a minimum he needed to shed at least 100 pounds. He seemed genuinely excited and eager to move forward. He verbally expressed his commitment to the task and promised that he would lose the weight.

Over the next 12 months I would check in with George via phone always asking about his physical condition. Every time I got the same response...that he was working on it. In my experience when someone decides to make such a dramatic life change such as the one George told me he was committed to you start hearing about diets, working out, running, new lifestyles, new friends from the gym, yada yada yada ... rather than "I'm working on it."

When October rolled around hunter George flew to Colorado, rented a car and headed to meet the outfitter at the trailhead. Upon his arrival I got a call from the outfitter telling me that hunter guy George showed up at camp tipping the scales just shy of 400 pounds (he weighed 350 or so when I met him a year earlier). By some miracle the outfitter managed to get him on a horse and into camp. The following day, day one of George's long awaited elk hunt, George called it quits claiming total physical exhaustion after less than one hour of walking and asked to be taken out of the mountains. I wondered then if I would ever hear from George again. It's been almost 10 years...not a word.

Hunter guy #2 I will call Bart (not his real name). Bart was at the time playing in the NFL (no, not that Bart). In short, hunter Bart got many of my same suggestions, as did hunter George, as far a physical preparation for the hunt. To look at him, Bart did not have an ounce of fat anywhere. This dude was ripped. He was proud of his athleticism and told me he consumed 6000 calories per day in the off season just to maintain his playing weight.  So, perfect physical specimen, hunter Bart heads out to elk camp that fall. Hunter Bart makes it for three hours before he is done in. When I asked the outfitter what happened? Did he get hurt? The response was simply that Bart was not prepared for the lack of oxygen at altitude and when combined with all the uphill climbing in the early part of the day, he just couldn't do it. Hunter Bart apparently knew his physical limits on the gridiron, but he was not prepared to expend the effort required to elk hunt at 10,000 feet. I'm

Jay Houston

sure I will hear from Bart again. He didn't strike me as the type of guy who would quit. He'll be back.

This entire chapter is essentially about one's ability to persevere and how important it is to every elk hunter's success: the steady persistence in a course of action, a purpose, especially in spite of difficulties, obstacles, or discouragement.

**Elk Hunter Tip: If you are in good elk country and all else being equal, the hunter who comes home with a cooler full of elk meat is the one who has learned the value of and actively practices mental and physical perseverance (Grit).**

Your physical preparation begins at home. Improving your cardio-vascular system, getting your lower body into shape and preparing for the effects of less oxygen are three critical aspects of your training. The amount of available oxygen at 10,000 is about 30% less than that available at sea level. That is like letting more than half the air out of one lung and trying to complete a serious all day workout...every day for the length of your hunt. I am not a trainer, but most gyms have a host of trainers whose sole purpose is to help you achieve your goals. Training is almost always easier if you have a workout partner. This may be your hunting partner, a neighbor or even your spouse. I would encourage you to seek out a gym friend who is already invested in you, someone who will encourage you to keep pushing through the tough times. It's about commitment.

In 2014 I decided that I was tired of being somewhat overweight. I didn't have a clue how to go about losing the weight as I had been somewhat lean most of my life. I did find a good friend at church who was in the same need of losing a few pounds. We both agreed to encourage hold each other accountable as we went through the weight

34

loss process. We committed the entire summer to early morning walks of two to three miles every day, and we determined to master the Paleo diet.

Raised a southerner I was a sugar junkie. Sweet tea, ice cream, sugar coated cereal, etc. The essentials for my weight loss plan was to avoid consuming any carbs and cutting out all processed sugar. Note: <u>Once your body learns that you are not going to feed it all that sugar and carbs it begins to acquire its fuel from your stored fat reserves</u>. In my case the transition for my body to start burning fat for fuel took about 10 days. By the end of the summer I had lost six inches around my waist. In the end, it really wasn't nearly as difficult as I had expected. My friend lost 40 pounds and I lost 30...meeting my goal. You can do this as well, but it is far easier if you do it with a friend.

I am not qualified to offer information on physical conditioning or weight loss. I can only encourage you to commit to a program that will insure that you are in the best physical shape you can be before you head to elk camp, if you are planning for success as an elk hunter.

**Preparing Financially for Your Elk Hunt**

I have said this a thousand times to hunters, "It always comes down to the money." Whether your hunt is the fully guided/outfitted version or the DIY (Do It Yourself) version, it always comes down to the money. Years of elk hunting experience confirms the fact that you get out of the hunt what you put into it. <u>There are no short cuts, which</u> is the premise of this entire book. As with your mental and physical preparation, you will also need to prepare your checkbook.

Any elk hunt is going to cost you more than you think (which is about twice what you will tell your spouse.) Let's take a realistic look at these costs.

**Cost of the Economy Hunt (100% on your own DIY elk hunt)**

For the purposes of expediency I am going to assume that our sample hunter does not live in elk country and will have to drive 3000 miles round trip (1500 miles one way). He will bring everything required for a one week stay in camp with him. We also assume that the hunter will be driving with a partner, and will drive straight through with no overnight stops to save costs. We will also assume that he already owns all of his personal gear and weapons and will not have to purchase them. The following are representative of the costs of a basic bare bones DIY hunt.

- Gas for the trip (@$2.50/gallon[2016], 14 MPG) 535.00
- Meals on the road for 4 days                                    100.00
- In camp food costs (per hunter)                             150.00
- Propane for cooking and heat                                  65.00
- Non-Resident Elk Tag/License                                630.00
- Adult Beverages (nice to have)                                75.00
- Game bags                                                              40.00
- Maps                                                                       40.00
- Unexpected stuff (nice to have)                             200.00
- GPS (nice to have)                                                 200.00

**TOTAL**                                                          **$2035.00**

Note: If you don't already own or have access to the essentials for a camp, plan on adding up to another $2500 to the above number for things such as wall tent, wood stove, cooking kit, water containers and purifier, tables, chairs, etc..

If you don't want to haul a truckload of camping gear to elk camp and if your checkbook can stand the additional hit, two highly recommended alternatives for the DIY hunter are drop camp hunts and private land

Jay Houston

trespass hunts. Either can increase your chances for success by as much as 25%. Drop camps average about $2000 per hunter while trespass hunts can run as high as $2600 per hunter depending upon the property. Look for more on each of these options in a later chapter.

**Drop Camp alternative total**                                   **$3728.00**

**Trespass Hunt alternative total**                          **$4328.00**

As you can see, the actual out of pocket cost of your DIY hunt can quickly add up. Honestly, there can be other expenses that I may not have mentioned that you need to consider as you plan for the success of your elk hunt.

**A Plan to Succeed**

Anything that's worth doing is also worth the time and effort spent to establish a workable plan. When we don't have a plan to succeed, by default we are planning to fail. Developing a well thought-out workable plan helps in numerous ways: (1) Distractions seem less distracting with a plan. (2) Your plan helps with navigation. (3) Your plan helps you to maintain focus and keeps you connected with your purpose...killing elk. (4) Every good plan takes into account alternatives for every step, every event. That way you are less likely to have to wing it. In the military I learned that no plan ever survives the first 30 seconds of contact with the enemy, but the process of having developed the plan leaves us far better prepared to adapt and get creative when the need arises.

One of the questions elk hunting clients usually ask is: should I buy a mule deer tag too in the event that I encounter a muley? Essentially they want to maximize their chances of harvesting an animal. My answer is designed to help the hunter maintain his focus. I remind them that their primary stated goal for their hunt is to return home with elk meat in a cooler. My council is that anything that distracts them from this goal, like hunting muleys while on an elk hunt, is counterproductive to their stated goal. If you want to whack a muley, make a plan and come back at a later date for your muley hunt. This can be a challenge at times as many hunters want to get the most bang for their buck. Some even want to have a bear tag in their pocket as well. More diversions..... FOCUS!

## Working the Plan

Evenings in elk camp around a hot crackling fire are, in my opinion, some of the best times. The camaraderie with hunting buddies, tales of the hunt and catching up since last season are but a few of those nuggets that make elk camp a magical place. Around the fire or over coffee at the end of the day in the cook tent, can also be an excellent opportunity to talk about the days hunt and update the game plan. Here you can learn from that day's experience and better prepare for following day.

**Elk Hunter Tip: Plans call for specific individuals to carry out specific actions in specific places at specific times. This allows everyone in the hunting party to know what is going on and how that can impact the group's hunt.**

Recently more and more of the hunters that I have talked to are military veterans who have served our country on multiple tours in Iraq and Afghanistan. **I thank each and every one for their service. I am honored to call them brother or sister.** They are the pros when it comes to hunting with a plan as they have learned to apply the lessons learned through training and experience in combat to their hunt. These men and women are intentional and purposeful. They all know well what happens when one goes into the bad guy country without a plan.

Jay Houston

Hunting in teams of two not only makes for a more enjoyable day afield, but it is tactically sound as well.

- Two sets of eyes and ears see and hear twice as much.
- Two collaborating intentional hunters can more effectively clear an entire drainage.
- Two hunters can more effectively block elk escape routes.
- Two hunters are much more likely to discover sign that elk are using an area.
- Finally, two hunters make field dressing and packing out your elk a much safer and less strenuous event.

**You Snooze You Lose**

The fact that you have taken the initiative to purchase and read this book in my opinion, places you in the top 10% of all elk hunters. Your effort to add to your knowledge base demonstrates your commitment, and commitment plays a huge role in your success as an elk hunter.

If you are hunting as part of a group that you have hunted within the past; you already know that not every member of your team shares that same level of commitment. Chances are that you are the guy who always plans the hunt, pre-scouts the area, interviews outfitters or consultants. Essentially you are the one who does the lion's share of the pre-event leg work. So you are the hunter that this passage is directed to because you have the ability to influence your fellow elk hunters.

If you want to increase your chances of success you need to get ahead of everyone else in the game. Just like in a NASCAR race, only the driver that crosses the finish line first gets the checkered flag and gets to drive into the winner's circle. Unlike T-ball, there are no prizes for second place. Essentially, if you snooze you lose. So how does this play out for the elk hunter?

39

**Elk Hunter Tip: A key tactic in your elk hunt strategy is that you should have your hunt planned and locked in AT LEAST one year prior to your actual hunt date.**

If you are planning to pursue trophy caliber bulls it may take you two years or more. This means that you will need to exercise whatever means of influence that you possess to get EVERY member of your hunting party on board one year prior to the hunt. Trust me, from years of experience this can be a real challenge.

When I first started elk hunting I hunted alone (not smart) and very little planning was required to get me into elk country. I knew very little about what I was doing, and the results were predictable....no elk on the ground. Over the years, I met others who shared this same passion for elk hunting and we began hunting together. At first there were two, then four and then....well in one year we went insane and had 19 hunters in camp. This was a train wreck with far too many hunters in camp, and I will never do that again. As you add hunters you add complexity and resistance to the communal effort, because everyone has an opinion on how things need to be run. Being the nice guy that you are, at first you allow everyone a voice to share in the planning until you discover that while everyone wants to be heard, not everyone is willing to carry an equal share of the load. So, let me help you out.

**Elk Hunter Tip: Become the team leader.**

Just suck it up and strap that leader pack on your back. Trust me, in the end this will save you a lot of stress and allow you to move forward with your planning and your hunt far more efficiently.

If you are planning a hunt either with an outfitter or on leased private property, the ONE YEAR RULE is critical. If that outfitter or ranch has a history of producing above average bulls you can bet that there are literally hundreds if not thousands of other elk hunters looking to lock in that same hunt or piece of property. If they do not have a history of producing, why would you want to hunt with them? In the days prior to the Internet, this time factor was not as critical, but today every hunter has virtual access to exactly the same information that you have. He doesn't have to call dozens of outfitters or ranch owners. All the information is readily available 24/7. Let me give you one brief example of the significance of good timing.

Every year Colorado Parks and Wildlife offers leftover elk tags. These leftover tags usually become available in midsummer. The actual date is published on their website at http://cpw.state.co.us/leftover. Experienced elk hunters who know the system are ready at their laptops as the deadline approaches. With leftover applications filled out online, including their credit card information loaded; their trigger finger is cocked and locked over the ENTER key as the clock ticks down to midnight MDT the night before the day when the leftover tags come available. At one second after midnight, thousands of ENTER keys are triggered all at the same time as each hunter rushes to be one of those fortunate few selected to receive a coveted leftover tag.

**Elk Hunter Tip: You snooze you lose**!

That's right, in less than five seconds it's all over. Your success depends on your commitment and determination to get there before the next guy. Consider elk hunter wannabe Late Larry.

Late Larry can mess up the entire planning process for the hunt. This is the guy who for whatever reason cannot get his act together. Everyone else in the group has committed. Everyone else has sent in their hunt deposit check. Everyone else has updated their work and family

41

schedule for the hunt. Late Larry seems to have one excuse after the other keeping him from committing.  Yet everyone wants Late Larry to come along because he is such a fun guy and an integral member of your group. What do you do? If this is an annual occurrence and Late Larry has done this in years past, you have probably decided that Late Larry's presence in elk camp is worth the risk. Great! Elk camp is as much about the camaraderie as it is about the actual hunting. Welcome friend Larry.

On the other hand, you may have to make a hard call if you believe that Late Larry's failure to commit is going to have an adverse affect on everyone's hunt if he doesn't get in the game.  More often than not, Late Larry's delaying tactic is about one thing... money. He either cannot afford the hunt, he didn't plan ahead to have the required cash when it was needed, or he hasn't worked up the courage to have a conversation about funding the cost of the hunt with "the boss."  If the latter is the case, you are out of luck if you want Larry to come along. If it is the former, consider asking the entire group to get together and see if there is some way the rest of the team might be able to come together to help Late Larry out of his cash flow crunch. Worse case, if all else fails, Late Larry might need to stay home.

Kevin Fair with daughters/hunting partners Shelby & Makenna

## Great Hunting Partners Produce the Best Hunts

The best elk hunter that I have ever known is my long-time good friend and former United States Marine Kevin Fair. Kevin is non-assuming, quiet, friendly, and has not a pretentious bone in his body. Kevin is also a living breathing encyclopedia of elk hunting knowledge; possibly having already forgotten more about elk hunting than I know. It's a good thing he doesn't seem to like to write; otherwise it might be his name on this book.

Some years back Kevin called and asked if I would like to come up to his [then] home near Granby, Colorado for an elk hunt. Kevin shared that he had access to some isolated tracts of rarely hunted private land that he said always held elk. In a heartbeat I accepted Kevin's invitation and began making my plan.

Kevin is a manufacturer's rep for a company that sells a number of lines for major hunting gear manufacturers. A lot of his time is spent traveling all over the country talking to hunters at shows about great products for his companies. Kevin's passion however, after his beautiful wife Cherlyn and their two beautiful and talented daughters Makenna and Shelby, is elk hunting and on this particular hunt, Kevin had generously invited me to tag along.

As I write this it dawns on me that this hunt was in 2006, ten years ago [2016]. It seems as if it was just yesterday.  Regardless, the memory of a great hunt is still vivid. **Elk Hunter Tip:  The memories we make are some of the best parts of elk hunting.**

Kevin and I were hunting Colorado's Third Combined Rifle Season. The ground we were hunting in the high country was covered in 8-12 inches of light snow with drifts as deep as 30 inches in places. The weather was crispy cold and the sky was clear and painted its customary Colorado blue.  The area we were to hunt was a very convenient 15 minute drive from Kevin's house.  Long before sunrise found us working our way up drainage in hopes of heading off elk Kevin knew would be moving back up mountain from feeding in fields below to their bedding areas in the timber.

Jay Houston

We decided to cross over to the opposite side of the drainage as we were hearing a bull bugle on the far side of the opposite ridgeline. As it was November 2, we both thought it odd that a bull would still be bugling so late in the season. The rut was more than a month past, but apparently this bull had misplaced his calendar as he had all of our attention. About halfway up the far side of the drainage, the bull bugles again, this time much closer. Since we were out in the open with little cover other than small sage clumps, Kevin and I just dropped and waited. In less than a minute the bull and two late season cows appeared near the head of the drainage. If this was going to happen it was going to happen right here and right now as there was no way for Kevin and I to close the distance without getting busted.

I was hunting with my faithful elk rifle, a Remington Model 700 LSS (Laminated Stock) chambered in .300 Remington Ultra Mag. My load was a factory 180 grain Swift Scirocco leaving the barrel at a healthy 3250 FPS while pushing 4221 Ft/lbs of Kinetic energy. At 500 yards (longest range in charts) the round was still traveling at 2325 FPS with 2160 Ft/ lbs of energy. My rifle was zeroed at 250 yards and was more than capable of delivering a knockout punch at 600 yards, that is if I was up to it, which Kevin and I were about to find out.

We both dropped down into about a foot of loose powder. Using both of our day packs as a rest since the shot was up hill, I began to settle into a prone position for the shot. Good fortune was smiling on us as the bull and his cows were taking a break in the open and had no idea we were there. At first I tried estimating the range visually but after dialing the scope to its maximum magnification of 12X and seeing a pretty small target, I quickly realized that this was going to be a long poke. I grabbed my rangefinder out of my coat pocket and tossed it to my Marine spotter/hunting buddy asking him to range the bull. After

45

what seemed like forever, Kevin looks at me with this questioning expression to tell me that the bull is out of range for my rangefinder. My thought, you have to be kidding me! Then it dawned on me that my rangefinder was a 2-3 year old model that maxed at 400 yards. Argh....! I had failed to plan for such a long range shot, but I did have a back up.

My pre-season homework and range work had revealed that the calculated bullet drop for my load was 27 inches at 500 yards which would require me to hold my crosshairs about ten inches over the bulls back. Estimating ten inches while looking through a scope dialed up to 12X with a Duplex reticle takes a bit of work. As I am not a trained sniper, this was about half head knowledge and half guess. More on this aspect of shooting later.

A mature bull elk has huge lungs. The double lung kill zone on a broadside bull elk is about 18 inches in diameter and the distance from the bottom of the brisket to his top of the backbone averages roughly 30-32 inches. Using a little Kentucky windage and my knowledge of the ballistics of the round I was shooting, I determined what I thought would be a reasonable holdover point for the shot, so I settled the crosshairs and took two breaths and let out half of the last one prior to touching off the shot. Kevin quickly told me that it looked like the round impacted about 5 yards in front of the bull. For whatever reason, they didn't even flinch. I racked in another round, added more holdover and broke round number two. This one, while failing to connect as well, definitely got their attention as it hit right at their feet, and in short order all three elk swapped ends and disappeared over the ridge.

Wondering how far of a shot it really was, Kevin and I took the time to range a small bush about a third of the way downrange, then walked to the bush and ranged the spot where the elk had been standing. The

46

combined total distance was 577 yards, easily the longest shot of my life. The elk were gone, but it was a great day to be an elk hunter. Tomorrow would be another day.

The following day was a combination of comedy and good fortune. We returned to the same drainage the following morning to see if we could figure out where the elk had gone the previous day. Much of the morning was spent team hunting the top and far side of the ridgeline above the point where I took my shot the day before. At some point, I discovered that I had lost my brand new [2006] flip phone somewhere on the hillside. While it was not the end of the world, it definitely was a problem. I remembered it being in my pocket until we had started up the last pitch. Kevin suggested that I backtrack and see if I could find it. He said he would starting calling it and to listen for the ringer. Thinking that I had likely shut the ringer off as I was hunting, I didn't have a lot of faith in this but, hey it was a $200 phone. I followed my tracks back about fifty yards and found a spot where I had stopped to take a brief break and there in about a foot of snow was a small pulsating blue light and my phone vibrating like crazy. Ahhh..... I was not going to have to go home and explain how I had managed to lose a brand new phone. Hunting with a buddy does have its advantages.

On we pressed for the better part of that day. Seeing no elk and no sign of elk in the area we began our trek back to Kevin's truck.

As we crossed the bottom of that same drainage as the day before and started the climb up the far side, Kevin happened to look back in the direction from which we had come. He taps me on the shoulder to hold up and turn around. There standing in the tree line at the top of the slope that we had just left moments before, but about 100 yards farther up the slope, stood a singular 6x6 bull casually watching us crossing the drainage. Knowing that time was short and he would surely not stay put forever, I slowly dropped to the snow again. Now I am lying across a downhill slope with a pretty severe 200-yard uphill shot at my two o'clock position before me. Resting my Remington .300 Ultra-Mag on my backpack again, I am trying to find a way to get the cross-hairs to calm down on the bull at this acute uphill angle.

 After two or three quick adjustments, I had to accept the fact that when I touched off the shot, there was a very good chance that I was going to get 'scope bit.' A scope bite, for the uninitiated, is when a shooter gets too close to the back end of the scope and is hit, usually just above the bridge of the nose by the scope from the rifle's recoil resulting in a perfect half moon shaped wound that bleeds...a lot.

With no time to range, I estimated the bull to be at 200 yards and touched off the shot. Three things happened: as expected the scope knocked the snot out of me throwing blood everywhere, the shot missed short and Kevin is saying shoot again, shoot again. So, I rack in round #2, settle in, move the crosshairs up a smidge and begin to break the shot # 2 just as the bull takes a step. Hastily I attempt to correct my point of aim to take into consideration the bull's movement and off goes round #2. The bull jumps straight up and swaps ends. He is clearly hit and runs downhill into a small patch of 8-10 foot tall new growth pines and disappears.

Kevin by now is rolling in the snow laughing his backside off as I now have two fresh scope bites and there is blood all over my face and the snow around me. For a minute or so, probably due to all the adrenalin there is no pain and we are high-fiving and laughing together at my unsightly state. I start packing snow on my face to slow the bleeding while we decide to give the bull some time to expire. As we can see

48

three sides of the patch of trees the bull has gone into we feel fairly safe in our assumption that he has expired right there. After about 30 minutes and getting me all cleaned up, Kevin and I head back up the far slope to the last spot where we had seen the bull. As we neared the bottom of the patch of new growth Kevin suggested I stay put in case he should jump the bull up high and it should come running out in my direction.

After about 20 minutes, my cell phone rings and its Kevin. He says that I need to come on up and the news may not be good. Argh..... I find Kevin standing beside a small diameter pine tree with a perfect .30 cal hole punched clean through it. The good news was that there was a lot of blood on the ground at the backside of the tree. As the sun was already setting we began a quick search of the immediate area. The blood at the tree was the only blood we could find. I went downhill and checked out the new growth where I thought the bull had gone....to no avail. As it was now almost dark, Kevin and I decided to call it a night and come back early the following morning to pick up the trail. Anytime a hunter has to leave wounded game on the ground overnight, it is going to be a long sleepless night. Mine was no different.

Early the following morning found us back on the same ridge at "the tree." After about an hour of searching for blood, other than my own, and finding nothing we both began to think that the bull had somehow made it over the back of the ridge and that we were in for a very long day if we were to find that bull. If I know for a fact that I have wounded an animal, I will do to almost anything to track that animal down. Leaving a wounded animal is not something I will do.

Having made up our minds to do whatever it took to locate that bull, Kevin and I started up the mountain in search of my lost bull separated

49

by about 50 yards. I had gone about 200 yards when I stepped into a clearing and there beside a blow down and facing me, unable to rise, was my bull...still very much alive but unable to get up. While I was elated to have found the bull without having to walk all over the mountain, I was devastated that my shot had been off and as a result this animal had suffered throughout the night at my hand. Quickly I said a brief prayer and finished what I had started the day prior. I hollered to Kevin and in minutes he was there offering congratulations for our success.

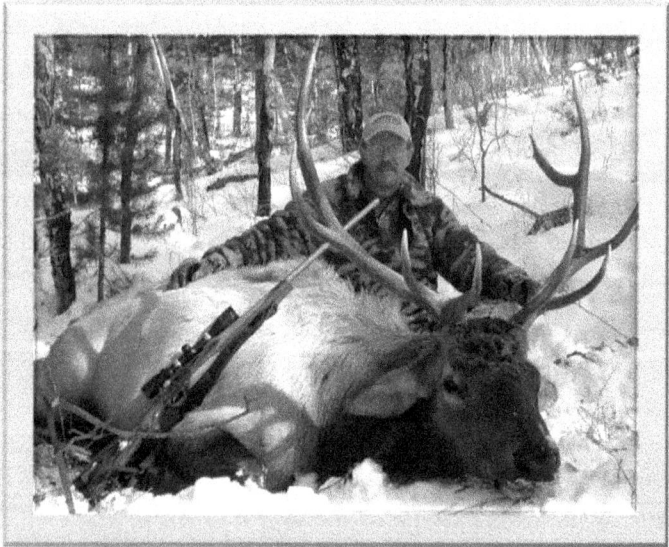

Jay, Colorado

We took tons of pictures and then began the work of field dressing the bull. I have to admit that most of the time we were working on the bull, I was dreading the hike back to the truck in deep snow with a couple of

50

hundred pounds of elk on my back. Finally, as were finishing the field dressing work and the meat was set aside in deep snow to cool; Kevin dropped an awesome surprise on me. He called a friend with pack horses, who rides in a few hours later to within 100 yards of our position and packs all the meat back to the truck. God is good and it was a great day to be an elk hunter with an awesome hunting buddy.

Note: Ensure that your rangefinder is adequate to cover any range that you might encounter. This would be a good time to replace the battery as well.

**Rob Springer, Kentucky**

## Silver Bullets on Elk Calling

If ever there was an elk hunting topic that has been hammered to death by TV hunting shows, journalists, and marketing types its elk calling. It is important to note that effective elk calling is an art that takes a lot of effort, practice and time to master. I do not think you can teach this skill from a book. Therefore I am not going to try; but I do want to share a brief thought with those who are toying with the idea of using a call for the first time in elk country. If you don't know how to use an elk call, in the field face to face with a hot bull is not the time or place to try to start learning.

Calling elk is not that different from calling turkeys. If you are a turkey hunter you know that most old Gobblers have been exposed to hunters calling them. As a result they are reluctant to respond to a novice who picked up his shiny new call from some big box store on the way to the turkey woods.

Calling however, can be a highly effective tool to have in your elk hunting tool box if you know what you are doing. I encourage you to spend time learning the how, when and where of elk calling long before you step foot in elk country. If you are a novice with a fair amount of practice under your belt, I recommend that you limit your calling to the occasional use of a cow call.

Cow calling can be advantageous in a number of ways. If you are trying to be sneaky and happen to break a branch walking through cover, a brief mew can serve to cover the mistake. Experienced elk hunters don't get too worked up over the occasional misstep. Elk make noise walking all the time. The cow call makes you sound more like the elk.

The occasional cow call can also serve as a locator call. When I am still hunting, I will throw out a series of cow calls and wait for a response as I am glassing an area. If I neither see, nor hear anything, after an hour or so, I will move on another 1000 (roughly) yards and repeat the process. The idea is to use the combination of optics and calling to increase the odds of locating elk in all that real estate around you.

Jay Houston

One of my long-time favorite cow calls is the Primos Hoochi-Mama. While it may not offer the flexibility of some other calls, this can be an excellent starter call for the novice as the mechanics are incredibly simple. Essentially, it is as close to an idiot-proof elk call as one can get. All you have to do is press down on the bulb with your thumb covering the small hole on top and out comes the call. If you press slowly you will extend the length of the call producing a less harsh sound and you will be less likely to spook nearby elk. The Hoochi Mama can be adjusted to reproduce the higher pitched sound of an elk calf by twisting the barrel of the call. In some cases this can produce a most dramatic result, as I am going to share with you now.

My wife Rae Ann and I had traveled to a ranch near the town of Delores in southwestern Colorado a few years back. Our plan was to use this opportunity as a much needed getaway from the world and maybe get in a little scouting of some prime elk country. We spent three days hiking and glassing while I crafted the beginnings of a plan for a future elk hunt.  Unfortunately, while we didn't eye any elk during our daily walkabouts, mule deer were everywhere. Rae Ann loves critters. I think she would have been content to stay out all night if there had been a full moon just to continue watching them. As it turned out we were in mountain lion country and my lion radar had the hair on the back of my neck come up a few times. So I suggested that we get back to camp before it got too dark each evening.

The last day of our short trip arrived all too soon. As we were driving out of the backcountry to a state highway, Rae Ann says "Jay stop....stop the truck." Her elk radar had gone off and she was anxiously pointing back over my shoulder to the far end of the meadow that was running parallel to the road we were on. To my surprise, about 400 yards away was a single cow elk, just standing there. Never one to let such an opportunity pass, I grabbed the Hoochi Mama off the dash and started doing my best to imitate a lost calf. Folks, you would have thought that cow had a cattle prod touched to her backside. She came running up the meadow as fast as she could stopping just 7-8 yards away on the far side of a three-wire fence that bordered the road. To say the least she was as worked up as any cow elk I had ever seen.  Since we were still in our vehicle she didn't identify us as a threat, but every time I would hit that calf call she went nuts running back and forth along the fence calling back to me. My thinking is that she was a cow without a calf and she thought she had found herself one. This calling back and forth went on for quite some time. Eventually her frustration got the best of her and she let out an alarm bark. She still didn't move away though. She just held her ground while looking in our direction. I continued to call back to her, and she continued cow talk with the occasional frustration bark but she never left. After a while another vehicle pulled up and she ran off. For a time, it was a heck of a conversation.  So what is the point? This event occurred in the middle of summer and we were on a public road in a vehicle. It just goes to show you that cow elk converse throughout the year and if you get their attention and prevent them from identifying you as a threat; it can work to your advantage.

*The best silver is not found lying around on the surface, you must dig for it. What gives it value is the time and effort required to acquire it. ~JH*

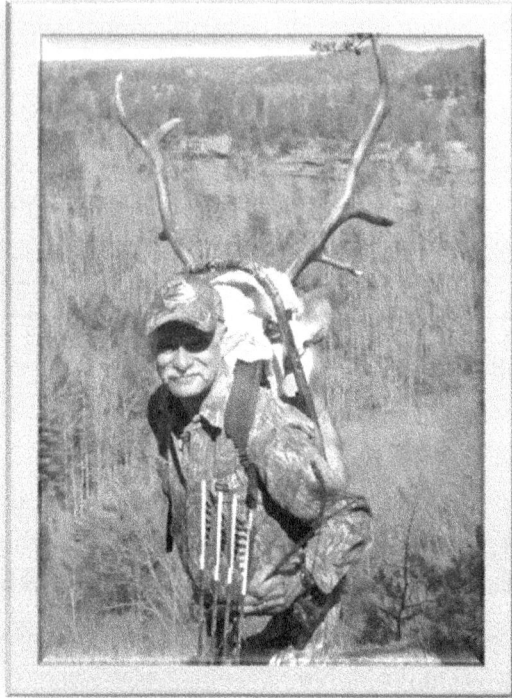

**Traditional Bowhunter & Good Friend Bill Carmen**

## Elk Hunting Fitness for the Young and Old
### by Bill Carmen

*This chapter was contributed by my good friend and a great elk hunter Bill Carmen. Bill has been slinging arrows at whitetails for over fifty years, and has bowhunted elk and other big game all over North*

Jay Houston

*America and Canada. In 2006, he became the first modern hunter to harvest a Kentucky elk with a traditional bow. Bill is a Regional Director for the RMEF. He lives with his wife Maureen in Versailles, Kentucky where he is teaching his grandchildren to hunt and fish.*

Earlier I talked briefly about the value of about getting in shape for your elk hunt. Recently I was having lunch will my good friend Bill Carmen, a die-hard elk hunter and a guy who believes strongly in the value of fitness training. I asked Bill if he would consider writing a piece on fitness for elk hunters. The following is Bill's generous contribution to this work.

**[Bill]** I hate to admit this, but I am sixty-five years old. Is it time for a rocking chair? No way! There are still a lot of critters to chase, mountains to climb, and rivers to wade. But, as much as I hate to admit it, I also have to slow down and change my approach to fitness. As a baby-boomer I know that I'm not alone!

I'm not a big, tough character. I was always the one who got sand kicked in his face, and I always envied the guy who had natural athletic talent. You know, the 4-sport kid who could set a long-jump record, and then go run a sub-50 440 with little or no conditioning. However, through shear stubbornness [GRIT], I have always been an athlete. I ran high school and college track, and as a young adult I was a bicycle road racer. For the past few decades as I have aged, my primary fitness goal has been to not only maintain my health, but to continue to go that extra mile in my hunting endeavors. But, aging certainly makes that more difficult.

I read somewhere that the number one complaint that western hunting guides express is the inability of their clients to close the distance to a bedded mule deer or bugling bull elk. The hunters arrive in camp unprepared for the rigors of steep terrain and high altitude. They are

57

either unable to climb into range at all, or they are so exhausted when they do, that they cannot steady themselves for an accurate shot. These hunters invest in travel, tags, and guide fees, but lack of fitness is often the difference between meat in the freezer and tag soup.

A few years back I was helping an elk hunter who was from out-of-state. We had passed up a smaller bull that morning and as we walked down an old logging road I stopped and bugled. Immediately, a bull answered from a gap in the ridge about a half mile above us.

"Let's go!" I said..."If we move up to the left, we can get in on him from down wind."

This guy made every excuse he could think of not to go after that bull. It was too late in the day, he'll be gone when we get there, he's the same smaller bull we just saw, it's too hot and the meat will spoil. It was a fairly steep climb, but there was no big hurry, and the bull might have been there we when arrived. We should not have passed on that bull. There is no guarantee that you'll kill anything. But there is a guarantee that you won't if you cannot go after the game. I told a buddy about that elk, he took a hunter up to that saddle and they killed a very respectable 350-inch bull.

Frankly, the very best way to prepare for a rigorous hunt is to regularly do a rigorous hunt. I reached out to my friend Steven Rinella, author and host of the *MeatEater TV* show. Steven is well known for his treks into remote wilderness areas to film hunts. I asked him if he had a secret to his fitness. Did he have a special training technique or an unusual fitness routine he might share? Here's his reply:

"I grew up hunting, fishing, and trapping in Michigan. There I learned to suffer, but I didn't learn how to handle long hikes and steep country until I moved to the Rockies. What I think of as backcountry or

58

mountain fitness came to me very slowly over the course of several years' worth of rigorous hiking in Montana. There was no secret to my development. I just got better and better the more I did it. It was kind of circular, really. I hunted in the mountains in order to get better at hunting in the mountains. There's really no other way to do it. That kind of strain cannot be replicated. Staying fit for the mountains requires being in the mountains."

Unfortunately, most of us do not have the ability to do rigorous hunts on a regular basis. We have jobs, family commitments, and we may not live near the mountains. Here are some tips that can help you prepare for tough hunts, and maintain overall fitness.

**Manage your time**. Examine your daily schedule to determine a good time to work out. Here's the most important part of that equation: Make that time period **sacred**. Do your absolute best to leave it alone. I still have a full-time job, so my three best times to work out are early morning, during the lunch hour, or early evening. It is a lot easier on my aging body to do two shorter workouts per day than one longer workout, so I do a 20-30 minute routine before breakfast and a longer workout at lunch. If I miss the morning or noon workout due to a work meeting or family responsibility, then I move it to early evening.

**Set Reasonable or Interim Goals**. If you are already fit and in pretty good shape, then your goal may be to do a wilderness backpack hunt in the Rockies after a month of training. If you are overweight and not accustomed to the rigors of a tough hunt, then start your training with plenty of time to meet your goals, and establish interim goals. Maybe, goal #1 will be to lose twenty pounds and walk for an hour. A later goal may be to lose ten more pounds, and walk for an hour with a full pack. The next goal may be to do a pre-season three day backpacking trip in steep country. Final goal- Be able to do your elk hunt in the Rockies.

**Stay healthy**. Avoid careless injuries like back strains and twisted ankles.....lift with your legs and watch your step. Eat, drink, and smoke moderately. If you smoke cigarettes, do everything in your power to quit. I occasionally smoke a celebratory cigar, but that's it. A cocktail, beer, or glass of wine at dinner is fine, but drinking too much will cause a hangover that causes you to miss your next workout. Over- drinking has other obvious implications....organ damage, auto accidents, relationship troubles. Enough said about that. Over-eating packs on the pounds which is the exact opposite of what you are trying to accomplish. Also, stay away from sick people. Last fall I was training for a difficult back-pack bowhunt. I shared a microphone at a conservation fundraiser with a guy who was sick. Of course, I caught his bug and lost several weeks of training. I did the hunt anyway, but really suffered on the climbs.

**Make it tough to say NO.** Keep your workout stuff handy, your shoes by the door, your bike road-ready, and your pack packed. It's a lot more tempting to hit the couch when you have to go to some effort to get ready to work out. Pre-plan options in case the weather is bad...keep your raincoat and rain cover for your pack, gloves and a stocking cap all easily accessible. Several years ago I bought an old beat-up mountain bike so I could ride in the rain without worrying about sliding on a slick road.

**Change up your workouts**. I like to do a hard workout every other day and an easier or different type workout on the off days. For instance, I may do a one hour hilly hike with a backpack on Monday, and a one hour hilly bike ride on Tuesday. Both are good cardio workouts, but they strengthen different muscle groups, allowing other groups to rest.

**Rest.** I like to take off a day or two a week. I work fundraisers on most Saturdays, so that's usually not a rest day. On rest days when I'm home, I may walk the dog, or go for a leisurely bike ride with the grandkids....just enough to loosen up....but the point is to allow your body to rest and recover.

**Get enough sleep**. Your workouts will certainly help you sleep better, but other things can affect sleep....eating dinner too late, alcohol, stress, a full bladder. I try not to drink fluids too late in the evening, as I wake up having to go to the bathroom. Sometimes I take a mild sleep aid, like Tylenol PM, but it is wise not to take too much of anything, as long-term use of even the mildest drugs can cause organ damage.

**Don't forget your upper body**. Swimming is a great cardio workout and helps maintain healthy arms and shoulders. Bowhunters are particularly susceptible to shoulder problems, and shoulders are probably the most important parts of an archer's structure. And yet we seem to neglect them until they give us trouble. I like to walk about a mile every morning before breakfast, doing a four- exercise routine with a ten pound dumbbell. Using the weight increases my heart rate and breathing, and the four exercises keep my shoulders healthy. Research has shown that even moderate weightlifting can lead to not just stronger muscles, but stronger bones as well. I look pretty silly walking around flapping my arms like a bird, but then again, I've really never given much thought to what people think.

**Engage in hunt-specific exercises**. As the date of your big hunt approaches, phase from general fitness routines to more hunt-specific exercises. Decrease your bike riding and increase your hiking with a full pack. I have a friend who secured permission to walk the steps in a twenty-three story building wearing a full back-pack. Another buddy walks the steps in the football stadium. Of course, the most specific exercise a hunter can do is to shoot your rifle or bow. Treat it just like any other exercise....shoot a lot one day and a little the next session. Bowhunters should change it up from hay bales to 3-D to stump shooting. Shoot when you are winded. Jogging from target to target on a 3-D archery course would be great preparation for a "run-and gun" bugling bull hunt. Do jumping jacks between shots at the rifle range. However, do not lose shooting focus. Concentrate on each and every shot.

**Listen to your body**. This is particularly important to aging hunter-athletes, but applies to everyone. Pay attention to subtle changes, aches and individual pains. They could be precursors to injury and may require changes to your routine or even simple modifications like arch supports for your shoes.

**Stretch and Warm Up**. This is something I'm always tempted to neglect, but I know I should not. Start each workout by stretching for a few minutes, and then jog or spin on your bike slowly until your muscles are warm and you break a mild sweat. Now you are ready to work out. This habit will prevent injuries.

**Stay hydrated**. Drink lots of water and sports drinks. Dehydration can lead to muscle cramps and injuries. A hydrated athlete can perform at his or her peak level. A good indicator of hydration is urine color. The darker, the more you are dehydrated, the clearer, the better.

Back in my old track and cross country days, we learned that one of the "gospels of running" was to **mix aerobic and anaerobic running**...and the same goes for hunt training. Aerobic exercise is where the athlete goes out for a long slow workout, like a 1 hour jog or a 2 hour bike ride in low gears, keeping a steady rhythmic breathing pattern. The old time runners know this as LSD, or long-slow- distance. An anaerobic workout would be shorter in duration, but higher in intensity, like a series of wind sprints or hill runs, or a 1 hour bike ride with steep hills or bursts of speed thrown in. This is called interval training. The philosophy is that early in your training period, do more LSD aerobic work, and as you near your big hunt date, do more interval training where you really get your

Jay Houston

breathing and heart rate working. A version of this type of training is "Fartlek," a Swedish word literally translated as "speed-play." Runners mix speed running with slow running. For instance, on a jog on a golf course, sprint from a tee box to a sand bunker, then jog to the green, then sprint to the next tee, never stopping, and allowing your heart rate and breathing to slow during the jogs. (Best done early in the morning when there are no golfers!) This can be done on country roads on a bicycle, using mailboxes and driveways as your sprint starts and stops. Do this spontaneously to make it fun.

**Running** should be the bread and butter of any fitness routine for the younger hunter. Just ask any U.S. Marine. However, for the older hunter-athlete it can be risky. Running can wear on knees, hips, and shins. If you are young and your joints are in reasonably good shape, there's nothing wrong with mixing in a generous dose of running with your other exercises. Just be prudent and pay attention to your aches and pains. Bicycling can achieve similar cardiovascular results, but has much less impact on your joints. I recently ran across a running journal I kept in college. Wow! Was I young and foolish! During one week in the fall of 1971 I ran nearly two-hundred miles. Two-hundred freakin' miles! It's no wonder my knees and hips are bad.

That brings up another good strategy to keep motivated. **Keep a workout journal**. Plan your routines and write down your goals, weekly workout schedules and what you achieved. It's cool to look back at a journal and see how far you've come.

Starting a new exercise regimen should begin with a **good physical exam by a physician**. A routine examination may reveal serious issues, or conditions that can easily be corrected. Blood tests might reveal that some minor tweaking of vitamins or medications could prevent complications and enhance you training.

**High Altitude** is something that you will probably encounter if you hunt in the mountainous areas critters inhabit. If you live in the East or at lower altitudes, you may need to engage in extra preparation for hunting at high altitude. Wilderness physicians have divided altitude into three zones. High Altitude is between 4,900 feet and 11,500 above sea level. Very High Altitude is between 11,500 and 18,000 feet. Extremely High Altitude is over 18,000 feet. Unless you are hunting Tahr or Argali Sheep in the Himalayas, you probably won't ever hunt at the extreme higher elevations. Most elk and deer are hunted at the High Altitude levels under 11,500. Mountain goats and wild sheep are sometimes found at the mid levels, above 11,500.

Twenty-five years ago I did a backpack archery elk hunt in the Weminuche Wilderness in Colorado. I was in great shape, and had hunted at 10,000 feet on several occasions with little trouble. On this trek, the trailhead was at around 7,000 feet. When we hit 11,500 feet, it was like I hit a wall. I was nauseated, weak, and listless [Symptoms of altitude sickness]. All I wanted to do was sleep. It took me a day or two to gain my strength, but I struggled during the whole time we hunted at that elevation. I shot at a bull mid-week and missed. To this day, I am thankful I did. Hauling elk quarters in that terrain at that altitude, for me, was out of the question. 11,500 feet was my limit.

The best way to combat the challenges of high altitude is to simply get in great shape. Try and plan your hunt so you can spend some time exercising at your hunting elevation early in the trip. Maybe you can stop at the summit of a major pass on your way to the hunt area and take a hike. For instance, there are a couple of high passes on I-70 and on Colorado 40 that would be excellent places to stop and hike for a couple of hours. If you live in the East, you might plan a weekend trip to a mountainous area in the Appalachians sometime before your hunt. For example, take your family to Gatlinburg, Tennessee to do the tourist

64

thing, and slip away for the day to hike near Clingmans Dome, the highest point in the Smoky Mountains. A nice weekend in Asheville, North Carolina could include some hiking on Mt. Mitchell, the highest point in the Eastern U.S. The Appalachian Trail is not too far from most Eastern U.S. locations, and has some great day hikes at reasonably high altitude. Anything over 5,000 feet will give you the altitude exposure that will help you acclimate when you actually start your hunt.

During your hunt, stay well-hydrated and eat high energy food. Take it easy the first couple of days, and do what you feel like doing. You will get stronger as your body acclimates. There are drugs that will help you acclimate, such as acetazolamide, commonly called Diamox. It is a diuretic, so it seems counterintuitive to take something that makes you lose water, but it reportedly works. However, if you choose to take it, try it in advance to make sure that it agrees with your system. I'm not much into taking any kind of drugs unless absolutely necessary, so I've never tried Diamox. Discuss this with your physician, and take it with caution.

**Lastly, have fun**! Formulate some entertaining adventures that can fit into your workout routine. This past winter I heard a rumor of some elk that were seen in a wilderness area outside of Kentucky's elk zone. The forest service road leading to the trailhead was closed for the winter, so I parked at the gate and rode my mountain bike to the trailhead, hiked in, hiked out, and rode back to my truck. I got in about ten miles of bicycling, and another seven or eight miles of hiking. Despite seeing no elk or elk sign, I saw some awesome scenery and had a wonderful day....and got in a great workout.

Once or twice a year I hike a couple of miles into a wilderness trout stream, fish upstream for several miles, and hike back out on another trail. It is a great workout and allows me to enjoy my other passion, fly fishing small streams. Maybe you like upland bird hunting. There's

65

nothing more fun for a shotgunner than walking all day with his or her best gun dog. What a great way to get some exercise and do something you love!

Back in the day (I sound like an old fart!) I was obsessive about fitness, and I worried if I missed a workout. I still use a disciplined approach to fitness, but now I don't freak out if I miss a session. Sometimes I'll put my pack down and enjoy the view, or I'll pull my bike to the shoulder of the road and snap a few scenery pictures.

On a personal level, the benefit of training goes far beyond being ready for that big hunt. Maybe it is the endorphins giving me that "runner's high." Smelling the new-cut hay on a cool summer morning bike ride, hearing the rhythm of my own breathing as I top that steep ridge, enjoying that spectacular view when I get there....those things are the path in the Japanese Garden, the means as good as the end. And, training makes me feel so darned good. If I miss a day or two, physically, I don't really feel bad. I may not sleep quite as well, but I don't feel much different. But, after that first workout when I resume my training, I feel absolutely great, like I had forgotten what I was missing.

 My bottom-line goal is still to stay fit enough to be able to haul a tree stand further, carry meat on a pack frame, chase a rutting bull, and take advantage of hunting opportunities that are out of reach for the average hunter. I encounter more game, see more scenery, and experience that occasional solitude for which we all yearn. As you age, fitness can enhance your quality of life, your health, and your enjoyment of the wild places we all love.

Jay Houston

## Closing the Deal on Distant Bulls

Almost every elk hunter, regardless of whether you are hunting the breaks of Montana or reclaimed coal mines of Kentucky has encountered a bull at a long distance and wondered what would be the best tactic for closing the distance for a shot without spooking the bull. While every situation is unique and will require you to adapt, the nuggets that I am going to share with you should increase your chances for closing on those distant bulls.

67

Jay Houston

**Rule #1: Don't rush it.** Unless spooked bad, elk will stay put in the same general area for hours, even overnight unless they are transitioning to or from their bedding or feeding areas. If you glass a bull grazing on a far slope, there is a very good chance that there is plenty of time for you to work up a plan of attack and close the distance for a shot.

**Rule # 2: Know and monitor the wind**. An elk's sense of smell is its number one tool for detecting a threat. Use whatever you have to monitor the wind whether it is a bottle of unscented talc or a small thread tied to your bow or the barrel of your elk rifle. Check it often.

**Rule #3**: **Visualize your Best Wind Route** taking the prevailing wind, thermals and terrain into account. Take note of visual landmarks (tall trees, dead trees, large rocks) that will help to keep you on course. Once you get off that high point and into the nasty stuff everything is going to look different. The large landmarks that you memorized can be your get well points as you move towards that bull. They also serve to let you know how close you are getting. Here is where a bit of technology can come in handy. Before you jump off the high point, you can use your Smartphone to take a picture of the landscape that you will be moving through focusing on the landmarks. This can serve as a way to jog your memory along the way.

When trying to close the distance on a bull, I always try to plan a route that will allow me to arrive at an initial shooting position roughly 200-300 yards downwind of the bull and whenever possible above him. Why above? In my experience, if a bull is going to blow out of there, more often than not they will run uphill making for the top of the ridge and the safety of the other side. The exception to this would be if your scent is what spooked him and it came from uphill. If you are a rifle hunter, this position may offer you a shot. If you are a bowhunter, this is where you will need to switch on your Ninja stuff to close into bow range. Notice I said close. This is where some bowhunters blow the stalk when they start calling. Leave the call in your daypack or pocket; if necessary ditch your boots. Again monitor the wind while you are closing on the bull. If the wind is swirling, I may check it every minute especially when I think I may be within 500 yards of the bull.

Taking all the above into account and your own physical limitations you will need to estimate how long it is going to take to move from your existing location to that of the bull. Keep in mind that the "best wind route" is RARELY a straight line. Many times your best wind route will be some portion of a great circle which can easily double or even triple the distance and time required to get in a good shooting position. While the straight line distance to the bull may be one mile. The circular route could result in a three mile or longer trek. Knowing this may tell you that you just cannot get there from here before you lose shooting light. In this case, your best bet is to note the bull's location and back out while making a plan to re-attack in the morning.

**Rule #4: Recheck the wind often**. In general terms wind moves down a slope in the early morning hours. Once the earth begins to warm in mid morning it will reverse and move back up the slope. That being said, remember that the wind in canyons and creek bottoms swirls a lot. A case in point, I was once stalking a herd bull we had nicknamed "the Growler" in thick dark timber on a bowhunt in the panhandle of northern Idaho. We were covered in scent masking stuff and one guy had even doused himself and a few of us with cow elk urine....which is really nasty smelling stuff! Anyhow, we could hear this bull bugling and were trying to pull him away from his cows using seductive calls...and it was working. We had successfully pulled this bull in from 500 plus yards to what we estimated to be less than 75 yards. We were able to discern this by listening to his constant bugling. As I was the shooter, I began setting up for what I hoped would be about a 50 yard shot. Suddenly the woods got quiet. After about a minute of silence, the bull sounded off again but he was clearly moving in the opposite direction. A quick check of the wind confirmed our worst suspicions that the wind has swirled and was now behind us.

**Elk Hunter Tip: We had become so focused on the bull and the setup that we failed to keep track of the wind. In just a matter of a few seconds it had changed 180 degrees and gone from favorable to busted.**

**Rule # 5: Manage your personal scent.** Bottom line is that all the planning, skill, practice and woodcraft in the world is not going to make up for poor personal hygiene resulting in a smelly hunter. Take care of it. If you plan on using a commercial cover scent, remember most of these only last about an hour. Unscented wipes stored in a Ziploc baggy are a great way to clean up some of your more nasty smelly areas.

**Rule # 6: Use Terrain Masking to your advantage whenever possible.** Creek bottoms, depressions, intermediate ridgelines, patches of timber can be used as a part of your game plan to close the distance. On cold days, air settles in the lowest areas. This can help to contain your scent as well as provide cover. Look for these types of terrain as you are planning your attack. Conversely terrain such as high rock walled creek bottoms that only a mountain goat can navigate may end your stalk before it gets started. Unfortunately, you cannot always see these obstacles until you are right on top of them. Been there...done that.

**Rule # 7: When in doubt back out.** I touched on this earlier, but in my opinion it is worthy of a little more attention. If the wind, terrain, remaining daylight hours, and your own physical condition are not conducive to closing the deal, this is when your good judgment comes into play. You should consider backing out and making a plan for a later time or looking elsewhere for another bull.

## The Elk Hunter's #1 Challenge: How to Locate Elk

Any experienced elk hunter will confirm that the single most challenging aspect of elk hunting is finding the elk. Long-time experienced elk hunters agree that it's actually about 80% of the problem. Unlike whitetail deer that may live and die on 100 acres or less, elk are always on the move. It is not unusual for elk to move as much as ten miles in a 24-hour period in search of food.

Jay Houston

Elk are opportunistic foragers, meaning that among other things they feed on whatever food is available. They are however continuously seeking out higher-quality food sources, especially in the fall of the year. Elk know that the cooler days of fall will soon be followed by the bitterly cold and harsh days of winter when food sources that were easily accessible to them in spring and summer will be covered with feet of snow. In order to generate sufficient energy to survive, their continued existence depends upon their ability to put on fat. This fat serves not only as an insulator against the cold of winter, but also a source of fuel for their body. Just like humans, when an elk's body can no longer find external sources of energy fuel, it will begin to use internal sources stored in the body's fat reserves. Thus, it is critical that the elk seek these high quality food sources wherever they can be found. If this fuel cannot be found in a particular drainage, they will continue to move until they find it. So, with elk in a continuous state of relocation, what tools can the elk hunter use to locate these elusive critters?

## Elk Sign, the Significance of Poop

One such tool is elk sign and the best elk sign is a fresh set of tracks...with the bull standing in them. This is the desired endgame. However, if you are in the process of locating elk, look for the signs of their presence or passing in the area. If there is no sign, it is likely that there are no elk in the area. Just like the large green signs on the highway that help us navigate from one point to another, elk poop or scat can help the elk hunter better understand how the elk may be using a particular area and where they may be found. Here are a few rules of thumb we can learn from elk poop. It's important to keep in mind that rules of thumb are general and not specific.

The texture and moisture content of scat can give the elk hunter an idea on how long it has been since the elk that deposited it was there. Soft

73

moist scat found on dry ground tells us that the elk was in the area likely within the past 12-24 hours. If it has rained in that same period, it may have been longer. Dry cracked scat tells us that it is been some time since that particular elk passed that way. Generally, I will crush a piece of scat with the tip of my boot. If it mushes out and does not break apart...that's a good sign that elk may still be in the area. Next, I look for color. Color can serve as an indicator of whether the elk are grazing or browsing. Elk favor grazing, i.e. eating ground grasses like cattle. However lacking sufficient graze they will switch to browsing from trees as do deer. Grazing can typically be indicated by scat that is greenish in color, while browsing results in a darker brown color.  Since elk strongly prefer grazing over browsing, if you find scat that indicates elk are browsing and if the ground is not covered in snow yet, chances are that those elk will not be in the same area for long as they will continue to move on looking for more nutritious forage.

Scat can also give the elk hunter an indication of the sex of the critter that left it behind. Cow elk poop is smaller than bull elk poop. It is shaped like a football tapered on both ends and is usually found in small piles. Bull elk poop is larger in size than that of cow elk and each pellet is usually flattened on one end producing a shape much like that of an acorn. Bull poop can be found in piles similar to that of cow elk or it may be clumped together. Some time ago I asked a wildlife biologist what caused clumping versus piles of individual pellets in bull elk. His response was that the clumping presentation reflects a less stressed elk.

**There is More Than One Kind of Elk Sign**
If you ask elk hunters to talk about "sign" more often than not the conversation will generally gravitate towards poop, but there are certainly other kinds of sign.

74

I like hunting creek bottoms because elk use active creeks as a water source and the forage available near water tends to be favored by elk. I have had some of my best encounters hunting creek bottoms late in the day as the elk begin to drift out of the timber and begin to feed and drink just before sunset. When you are scouting creek bottoms look for small areas in the stream where the silt on the bottom of the stream has been disturbed. The water will be murky rather than clear. When elk drink they often stand in the water which results in a disturbance to the stream bed causing cloudy or murky water. An alert keen-eyed hunter will notice the disturbance and begin looking for game trails that lead to that point from the timber. He then back tracks to gain an understanding of how the elk are accessing the water source and uses this information to develop a plan to ambush the elk. If you locate cloudy water in a particular spot of a moving stream, it might be time to slip your safety off or notch an arrow.

**Here's Your "Elk" Sign**
Elk bedding areas can be excellent sources of sign. If you happen across a bedding area here are some things to look for. Cow elk are communal and typically bed nearby one another often just a couple of yards apart. So you can expect to find the depressions where they lay bunched up. Bulls on the other hand prefer to have some space so look for depressions that are separated from the primary group. Usually the bulls will lie within 20-30 feet of the group of cows.

Elk bed daily as a way to rest and digest. The digestion part requires water so look for bedding areas in relatively close proximity to some type of water source. Look for springs and seeps within the cover of timber. While harder to find, these offer an excellent source of water and they offer a more secure source so the elk do not have to venture out into the open.

Jay Houston

When you gotta go, you gotta go. When elk arise from their bed as they do multiple times throughout the day, they often urinate. For reasons that should be obvious cow elk will urinate on the border of the bed depression while bulls urinate more towards the center. If you happen upon a single elk bed check for dampness around the edges and in the middle. This sign may give you an idea if the bed was that of a bull or a cow.

**Glassing for Elk**
Glassing for elk from a high point with a good spotting scope or high quality binoculars cannot be over emphasized. When I expect to be doing a lot of glassing, especially if I am hunting a new area, I will carry a small light-weight collapsible tripod in my daypack. Most spotting scopes come ready to mount to a tripod; binoculars typically require some sort of adapter which means extra weight. If I'm going to use binoculars I use the top of the tripod as a rest without the fuss and extra weight of an adapter.

The true value of glassing is that it allows the elk hunter to search out distant slopes and tree lines without the risk of busting the elk that may be present by accidentally stumbling on them. Elk hunters that are not familiar with glassing and its value are usually those that drop out of the hunt early due to exhaustion saying that the only elk they saw all day were hauling buns over a far ridgeline.

When glassing, focusing upwind is preferred because any elk you may spot downwind will not remain there for long. Let me share a brief story that I believe will help to make this point.

It was the first rifle season in Colorado and I was solo hunting. I had been glassing a small herd of mostly cows that were feeding in the open about 100 yards from a tree line. I was hoping that the tree line would eventually produce a nice bull. I estimated that the elk were almost a mile from my position hidden in a small pile of boulders that offered excellent views over almost 180 degrees. My elk hunter's gut told me that if I was patient, there was a good chance that a bull might show himself sooner or later. So I had committed myself to waiting him out all day if necessary.

I had been glassing this herd for nearly an hour, always keeping an eye on the wind direction which had continued to be favorable. Other than the occasional inquisitive look around, the cows appeared to be content as they grazed. Unexpectedly, one of the cows, probably the old lead cow, pops her head up and looks in my direction. Shortly thereafter, another head, then another, until all of the cows had stopped grazing and were looking in my direction. As one they all swapped ends and trotted into the safety of the tree line and out of my sight. A quick check confirmed my suspicion. The wind had indeed shifted and had placed me upwind of the elk's position. Even at a mile's distance the elk were able to detect me. **Lesson learned:** closely monitor the wind to make sure you are always downwind of the elk.

You may recall in the story above I talked about the P word...PATIENCE. To give emphasis: synonyms for patient include: long-suffering, uncomplaining and enduring. At my age, there is probably an entire chapter I could write about the topic of patience and its many virtues...but I won't make you suffer through that. What I do want to emphasize is that those long hours spent glassing can be far more productive for the elk hunter than time spent wandering around aimlessly telling yourself that you are elk hunting. There is, in my opinion no method of locating shootable elk more efficient than glassing.

77

Jay Houston

**Locate the Food, Locate the Elk**

The number one item on an elk's checklist of priorities is locating and consuming food of the highest nutritional quality available. Outside of the rut, ninety percent of an elk's day consists of feeding, digesting and resting. While other needs may rank high, absolutely nothing supersedes an elk's dietary requirements. Not security and not breeding...survival is about food. Without the essential nutrition elk acquire by feeding, all else is pretty much a moot point. If you are serious about elk hunting, you should get serious on learning their feeding habits.

In all the years that I have been elk hunting, I have yet to knowingly run into a hunter in the field that could tell me, by name and sight, which plants that elk prefer to feed on. While I am sure that there are many hunters that do possess this information, I offer that they may be the exception rather than the rule. Therefore this discussion will focus on elk feeding habits, including the differences between the feeding habits of bull and cow elk. By understanding the specifics of how and why elk feed as they do, it should lead us to a better understanding of the elk, which hopefully will allow us as hunters to better predict where elk will be at a given time.

When planning a future hunt the smart hunter should factor into the plan two established aspects of elk behavior. First, elk are exceedingly opportunistic, meaning that they are adaptable and will whenever possible take advantage of favorable situations. It is this opportunism that has caused elk to become such a migratory creature seizing upon a variety of food sources. How does this play out for the hunter?

In the fall, as forage with the high nutritional value elk require to make it through the rut and the following winter months becomes more and

Jay Houston

more scarce, the elk are motivated to continually travel to new growth food sources as they become available. They will exploit these until the food source is depleted or other factors such as extreme weather or predators force them to move on. Sources of new growth forage change as the season's progress from late August into the early winter months. In late August and early September, new growth can still be found throughout most elk summer range in open grasslands, moist secluded forests, near valley floor seeps, and along water sources near the heads of drainages. It is this broad dispersal of food sources with a high nutritional value that determines why elk may be in one particular drainage today and in a different drainage tomorrow.

Once the frosts of mid to late September begin to take their toll on the quality of food in a particular area, the elk will move again in search of quality forage. When adverse weather, either too warm or too cold, moves into the area, elk herds usually break into smaller groups. They will quickly seek the late season new growth and security that can be found on the forest floor in heavily timbered tracts. These also offer a protective thermal barrier from the effects of the weather. This shift from open area grazing to forests is usually abrupt because it typically coincides with the beginning of hunting season. While hunting pressure is a factor in the transition, research indicates that this movement is related more to the availability of forage with high nutritional value and changes in temperature. As freezing nights take their toll on grassland food sources, the elk will transition from grazing to browsing, and their use of forested areas will increase. Concurrent with the onset of hunting season is the rut, which throws a wrench into the normal foraging patterns of the elk. Bulls and cows alike are required to put reproduction on the front burner for a short period of time. It is during the rut that bulls may burn off as much as thirty percent of their

79

accumulated body fat herding and breeding. This often leaves them in a severely energy depleted state going into winter.

Following the rut, with the possible exception of a few younger bulls, the cows and bulls begin to separate. Studies suggest that it is the bulls that choose to leave the cows. Factors that influence this decision can include the following: 1) that bulls, having expended large amounts of energy, must spend most of the time remaining to rebuild fat stores before the deep snows of winter arrive. To avoid competing for essential forage with the cows, whose reproductive priorities are to optimize security for calves over quality forage; the bulls depart the herd for areas where competition is less. Larger more mature herd bulls that have expended more of their energy and fat reserves, usually seek the best opportunities they can find for food, as well as refuge from hunters, in secluded forested tracts at the highest elevations. 2) Another factor for this dispersal of cows and bulls is predation. As the snow level gets deeper in the high country an elk's ability to flee is impaired and antlered bulls in a herd of cows easily stand out to predators. By remaining with the herd they risk becoming a target, especially older bulls. As a result, bulls will separate from the cows and seek out more secluded feeding and bedding areas. 3) The lives of elk revolve around what Thomas & Toweill in their 1982 volume, *Elk of North America; Ecology and Management* refer to as the Law of Least Effort. This means that the necessary resources that elk require must be obtained with a minimum of effort in order to maximize the benefits derived. This rule is predominant in elk behavior and is evidenced by the amount of time elk invest in eating and resting as discussed earlier. The balance of their day, ten percent or less is spent standing and walking around usually in close proximity to their bedding areas. The objective is to store up as much energy and fat as possible, while burning minimal

Jay Houston

calories. Elk behavior in winter such as walking one behind another in deep snow, feeding in softer shallow snow, or migrating to lower areas where they do not have to work as hard to feed is evidence of this.

For years I failed to give much attention to the differences in the feeding patterns of cow elk and those of bulls. In most cases during the hunting season, when we ran into a mixed herd of elk, i.e. cows and bulls, I was more focused on getting setup for a shot, and never gave their feeding habits a second thought. In recent years, however, with the heavy increases in hunting pressure on public lands, finding the elk has become the #1 challenge. Like most hunters, when the elk began to become scarce, we applied what might be called a brute force strategy, i.e. hunt harder and hunt longer. Unfortunately this strategy failed to produce the expected result. It was this failed strategy that I have witnessed or learned from year after year in camp after camp that brought me to the point of examining how most elk hunters hunt and what can be done to help them become more successful. If you want to get into the elk, you have to hunt smarter! If we want to become more successful elk hunters in an ever-increasing environment of high-pressured elk, we will have to learn more about the elk themselves.

### Different Feeding Habits of Bulls and Cows

So how is a cow elk's feeding habits different from that of a bull? Due to the cow's role in reproduction, cow elk have an enhanced ability to acquire and store fat and nutrients from the forage they feed on during summer and fall. As a result of her increased ability to store fat and nutrients, the cow is not as dependent on high quality feed and thus can ingest more fibrous material than a bull during long winter months. Therefore she is not as pressured to continually seek out new high quality food sources, and because of her reserves, she will not have to feed as much or as often in winter. Not having to focus as much on forage, a cow's time is spent more on protecting her calf from predators. Large cow-calf herds that gather for mutual security and are observed in elk country throughout the winter are a great example of this.

Bulls on the other hand, especially the older mature bulls sought after by hunters, must pack away all the high quality nutrients they can find. The average bull will consume as much as twelve pounds of forage per day. If he hopes to survive the extreme temperatures of high country winters, avoid predators, and play his role in maintaining the gene pool, he must focus his post rut efforts on maximizing his intake while minimizing his exertion; again the law of least effort. As a vital player in the future of the gene pool, he must not compete with the cows that are responsible for producing and protecting the next generation. Due to his larger body size and antlers, the bull can afford to trade off security for forage. Soon after the end of the rut, the bulls begin to drift away from the cow-calf herd in search of sources of nutrient rich food. Less mature bulls may be found in small bachelor groups again as they were in summer if the forage is plentiful, but older larger bulls become quite solitary and reclusive.

Because of their larger body size and its ability to absorb more heat, bulls must disperse significantly more retained heat than cows. This requirement causes bulls to seek out cooler areas in which to feed and rest such as dark timber, blow downs, and shadier North facing slopes on warmer days or days of bright sun. Typically larger bulls are the last to evacuate the cooler high country when winter snows begin to accumulate.

Jay Houston

I have been asked, "How much snow does it take to move elk out of the high country?" My hip pocket response is that when the snow depth begins to come up to an elk's belly, they start looking for an easier place to find lunch. For cow elk this may be 14 to 18 inches while for bulls it may take as much as 24 inches of snow to move them to another area. Keep in mind that there are no hard and fast numbers on this and that other factors may affect when elk begin to move down the mountain (migrate) in search of an easier to obtain meal.

When it comes to the types of habitat in which we can expect to locate elk, one that seems to generate a fair amount of discussion is that of small burns, i.e. areas that have been burned over in a forest fire. Burns can play a vital role in the ecosystem for elk, though perhaps not as vital for cows as for bulls. Nutrient rich forage in burn areas can begin to reappear in only a few months following a fire. The tender new shoots tend to attract elk for as much as three years following the fire. Small burns offer bulls a source of quality nutrients for building fat reserves and minerals for antler development during the summer. In the fall these same areas provide excellent forage that help bulls make it through the winter. Because of the open area herding behavior as a form of protection against predators, cow elk do not frequent small burns as much as bulls.

Time spent feeding and bedding represents roughly 90% of an elk's day. Prime daytime feeding for elk is the first few hours after sunrise and the last few hours before sunset, while bedding takes up the majority of the time in-between. This schedule changes dramatically, however, during the rut. As both cows and bulls are focused on reproducing, much of the time otherwise used for bedding is now spent traveling or standing. Feeding continues to take up the majority of a 24-hour period, but

Jay Houston

rutting and rut related activity seems to override the need for sleep, especially for bulls. In the normal course of a 24-hour period, elk will feed and bed both day and night. During summer months the feeding patterns of elk remain about the same with regard to daytime or nighttime feeding. However, the amount of time that they spend bedding at night almost doubles from 20 to 40% in winter as the elk attempt to optimize the use of every available calorie...again... the law of least effort.

**The Best Times of the Day to Hunt**
Hands down my all time favorite time to hunt is immediately following inclement weather, especially if it was a lengthy snow storm and the outside temps have dropped significantly. Following storms, elk begin moving out of the cover that they have holed up in. If it was a lengthy storm, i.e. all day or more, you can bet that they are hungry and it is this hunger that can work to the smart elk hunter's advantage. Chances are a lengthy storm has kept the hunter in camp as well. Smart elk hunters are always looking out for signs of clearing weather. As soon as you see that line of clear sky coming in from the west, it's time for you to head out. Yes, even if snow is still coming down in buckets. You want to be hunting right after the storm stops as the elk will start filtering out of cover within minutes.

The fresh snow also aids in your stalk as it allows you to move virtually silently. An old time elk hunter taught me this lesson as we were holed up in his pickup waiting for a severe hail storm to pass over. We had been in the truck with the heater going full bore for almost an hour and it was getting late into the afternoon. I was getting truck fever just wanting to do anything but stay in that truck. The old hunter encouraged me to be patient. As the trailing edge of the storm passed he told me to keep my eyes on the tree line about 500 yards in front of us. Sure enough, it wasn't five minutes after the storm passed that the elk began to filter out into the meadow and begin to feed. Unfortunately for us, we were trapped out in the open with no way to approach the elk unobserved...so I just observed and learned. Since that time, whenever I see a storm coming I just hunker down and wait it out. If it looks to be a brief blow, I look for a large conifer and crawl in underneath the low hanging branches. I can remain completely dry in such a way while rain, sleet and snow come down like it is the end of the world. When it stops, I'm huntin'.

Successful big game hunters know game tends to move more in the early hours of morning and just before dark. In the morning elk are returning to their bedding areas after a long night of feeding. They are singularly focused on moving from point A (their feed area) to point B (their bedding area). The elk hunter who can place himself along this path creates an opportunity for himself. The key to making such an ambush work is timing and determining how far up the mountain to place your stand. Too low and the elk pass by before legal shooting hours. Too high and the elk may stop short to bed down. When elk are moving up the mountain and I am hoping to set an early morning ambush, I am always on the lookout for good shooting lanes in cover. Don't look for elk to move out in the open. Even under cover of darkness, elk prefer to move inside of cover.

Another favorite time to hunt is the last hour before dark....more so even the last 15 minutes if you are hunting in an area that is heavily pressured by other hunters. In the evening, elk move out of the timber and begin to drink and feed. If I had to choose, I would pass on a morning hunt, try some really sneaky bedding area hunting during the middle of the day, and then focus my effort on bagging a bull just before dark. The "just before" dark is important for a few reasons.

85

Jay Houston

Darkness is a time of predators and an elk's threat awareness goes to its highest level once it's completely dark. The last 30-45 minutes of daylight encompass the time when the elk come out to begin to drink and feed. Their vision is not yet restricted by darkness so their threat level is somewhat lower. The elk hunter with good low-light capable optics who is already in place can use this time to his or her advantage.

**Elk Hunter Tip: An evening hunt during the last minutes before legal shooting light ends can be magical if you are prepared. Outstanding low-light optics can make the difference between enjoying backstraps for dinner, and making do with reheated chili.**

Whether you are a bowhunter or a rifle hunter, I strongly recommend that you invest in the best low light optics you can afford. There are few things more frustrating than having made a successful stalk only to discover that you cannot close the deal because you cannot clearly see your target through your scope or your bow sight. As I am primarily a budget sensitive rifle hunter, I really like Nikon and Leupold optics for their excellent low-light capability.

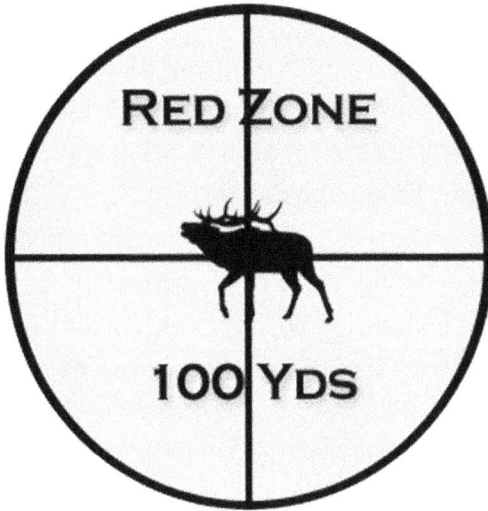

## Own the Red Zone / Controlling the Battlespace

The Red Zone is where all the planning, all the practice, all the strategy and all the persistence culminate. This is where you find out if all of your preparation is going to pay off. The Red Zone is that space inside a 100 yard radius circle around the bull. If you watch sports on TV, there is a show entitled the Red Zone®, where all the touchdown or basket scoring activity in a particular game is shown one play after another. The Red Zone is where we as hunters close the deal.

87

**Elk Hunter Tip: The true value of the Red Zone is in the hunter's ownership of the space.**

In the military we called it control of the Battlespace or of the Airspace. He who controls that space has the advantage. Far too many elk hunters fail to adequately appreciate this truth. By way of example, when a soldier is in territory believed to be held by the enemy, his level of alertness and caution are very high. But when that same warrior moves into a town known to hold enemy combatants intent on his destruction or that of his team hidden behind every wall or doorway, his intensity level goes off the chart. Every shift in the wind, every misplaced rock, every sound, every shadow, every smell is processed in milliseconds as his survival, that of his team and success of the mission depend upon it. Inside the Red Zone, while our lives may not hang in the balance, we should be at a similar level of alertness if we expect to be successful elk hunters.

Ownership of the Red Zone is about focusing all of our senses, all of our skills, and of our experience into that space and that mission...locating and killing the bull.

**Do's and Don'ts within the Red Zone**
- Take care of bodily functions prior to entering the Red Zone
- Actively monitor the wind direction
- Select a stand with unquestionable concealment
- Minimize all sound
- Pre-Identify clear shooting lanes
- Pre-Range all landmarks within each shooting lane
- Breath through your nose
- Empty your hands except for your weapon
- Remove sunglasses

- Minimize verbal communications with others, use hand signals only if required
- If bowhunting, have a plan on when to draw without detection (critical). Generally, if you cannot see his eyes, he cannot see you.
- If rifle hunting, assume your optimum shooting position with a rest whenever possible
- Turn off ALL sounds (including text and email) to cell phone (OFF beats setting to silent) and radios
- Open or remove lens caps on scope
- Insure scope is set to lowest magnification for the situation
- If you are using a Bullet Drop Compensation (BDC) type scope reticle, KNOW the subtention marks/ranges for all magnification settings...yes they change when you change the magnification setting. If necessary, use a dope card.
- Insure a live round is chambered and safety is on.
- Nock arrow or place your release on D-loop
- Remove boots if necessary to reduce noise
- Minimize detection by avoiding use of calls inside 100 yard range
- Minimize detection by avoiding any movement inside 100 yard range
- Don't smoke, chew, dip, eat, drink, sneeze, belch, or fart
- Move your eyes before you move your head
- Don't forget the wind.

**Last Ditch Tactics Inside the Red Zone**

When nothing else is working and I have decided that I will do anything to close the deal inside the Red Zone, I have a few hip-pocket plans that I use. Granted they work less often than not, but that is why they are called last ditch tactics.

1. If you cannot close on a bull inside of 100 yards and you cannot get him to come to you, try this: Pull out your handy bugle and **GO LOUD** right in his face giving him your best imitation of a young raghorn that has managed to sneak into his man cave undetected. A young bull's bugle often sounds more like a whistle. There are no chuckles at the end and usually only one octave rather than the more conventional three octave rising bugle. Sometimes this can shock a herd bull into a senseless rage causing him to throw caution to the wind and come charging right at you. The key here is to be quick, loud, and ready for anything. You might want to have a good size tree that you can get between you and that bat-crap crazy bull.

2. If you are in the Red Zone and cannot close the distance and you have no cover, I have seen other hunters successfully close the distance by simply **RUNNING** directly at the bull across open ground stopping only to take the shot. Is this nuts? Probably but on rare occasions when nothing else will work, you might give it a try.

3. **BACK OUT**...try again tomorrow.

*"The only thing necessary for the triumph of evil is for good men to do nothing."*~Edmund Burke

## The Silver Elk Hunter

*"Was not this ... what we spoke of as the great advantage of wisdom -- to know what is known and what is unknown to us?"* ~ PLATO

The Silver (over 50) elk hunter has a clear advantage over our younger brethren. We have already wooed and won our damsels; chased and slain our dragons; and are now in the process of enjoying the absolute

91

Jay Houston

joy of being alone in that part of God's great outdoors called elk country. We have learned that we have nothing to prove to anyone but ourselves.

Anyone that has been on an elk hunt can attest to the fact that it is one of the most physical hunts you can attempt in the lower 48. A typical wake-up arrives around 4:00 AM and if you are lucky you may collapse back into your sleeping bag at the end of the day by 10:00 PM. A little math confirms that you can be on the go for as much as 18 hours a day. That means that you can be hunting day after day with just six hours of sleep a night. For twenty and thirty something's this may work, but for those who look back upon the 50 year mark, quality rest becomes more of a requirement than a luxury. Eating smart and hydrating regularly also move higher up the list of one's priorities in order to replenish burned up energy reserves and replace fluids in the silver elk hunter's game book.

*"Old age and treachery will always beat youth and exuberance."*
~ David Mamet

Reality check: If you are over 50...you are likely not going to be able to keep up the same pace in elk country as you did when you were in your mid thirties, so don't try. There are times when brute force may be required, and there are times when hunting smart works even better.

A few years ago, I accepted an invitation for an archery elk hunt in the rugged St. Joe National Forest in the Idaho panhandle. All of my hunting partners including the guide were in their mid to late twenties. I was in my early 50s. Upon arrival at our remote camp I quickly determined that

92

this was going to be a physically challenging hunt. The only piece of flat ground was the small area where our base camp had been setup. Every foot in any direction outside of camp was steep with slopes covered in thick Alder. Uphill climbs required pulling oneself up the slope hanging onto whatever you could grab one step at a time. Downhill was tougher as all that brush that we had used to climb up the hill served to wrap up our boots making for some rough going. My knees took a real beating. My younger hunting partners were like mountain goats, surefooted and ignorantly fearless beyond reason. Early on I made a decision that if I was to persevere for the entire week; I would have to hunt on my own terms and at my own pace. So I decided to slow down and take my time. Initially the youngsters would look back at me with their "are you ok" look. But before long they decided to just leave me alone. As a result of my slower pace, I was the one who actually heard and located the elk before the rest of our group in many of our encounters. I was also the only hunter in our group to have a shot.

**Elk Hunter Tip: Go slower...move quieter...see more elk. Live to tell about it.**

The following are just a few of the benefits to being an over 50 elk hunter.

- **You learn to enjoy the journey**. Just the other day as my son-in-law Jon and I were driving to a local firing range to burn up some lead, he asked me about my time flying fighters in the Guard (ANG). As anyone who has not lived that life, his questions were quite valid. He asked me about my former fixation on going low and fast. As I talked Jon through the adrenalin rush of flying just above the treetops and through mountain valleys at 540 knots, it dawned on me how much I

93

have changed and how far I had come in the past 20 years. In those early years my life, like my profession, was all about leaping from one adrenalin rush to the next. I always seemed to be in a hurry. Yet sometimes it seems I was living without direction. We had a saying, "Speed is life." Now I have learned...Family is life.

- **You learn to hunt smarter.** Silver elk hunters savor the serenity of a crisp fall morning preceded by a cacophony of bugles that magically ceases before sunrise...and we are ok with that. One of the real joys I've experienced while elk hunting is trying to outsmart the elk. Again, I have the advantage over my more youthful hunting partners as my 63 years of knowledge easily exceeds what I knew 25 years ago. Please do not get me wrong, I know some very successful elk hunters who are not even 40. I wish I still had some of the physical attributes of these 30-somethings.

- **You learn to pay attention to the details.** I recall a truth that I learned some years ago from reading Michael Dell's (Dell Computers) *Direct from Dell: Strategies that Revolutionized an Industry.* Please accept my paraphrase but the essence of this nugget was that Dell attributed much of his business success to his near fanaticism in paying attention to the details. While fanaticism might be somewhat overkill for elk hunting, I wholeheartedly agree with Dell's assessment on the value of paying attention to detail.

When I was younger we had another saying: *"There are two rules in life (1) don't sweat the small stuff; (2) it's all small stuff."* Sounds innocent enough doesn't it. Do not believe this. When one adopts this world view, one ceases to give due diligence to

94

the details in life that make all the difference. Once I shed this and begin to focus on identifying and managing the details, things began to change....for the better.

The Silver Elk Hunter knows the value of paying attention to the small signs left by elk. Taking the time to pattern the elk movements in your area, knowing your chosen weapon intimately, and providing your body with quality nutrition are just a few of the details that can make all the difference between elk meat left walking around in the timber and elk meat in a cooler.

- **You learn to master your weapon of choice rather than settle for mediocrity.** For many years I have enjoyed bowhunting elk as well as rifle hunting. However, it seems that in today's big game hunting world one is encouraged to choose one method over the other. For the most part, I think this is merely a marketing strategy designed by product manufacturers to motivate the elk hunter to spend more and more on new gear. In a way, if we look at the high costs of gearing up that seem to increase exponentially every year, I can see where picking one method might be a lot easier on your wallet.

Many of my conversations with elk hunters eventually get around to bows, bow sights, rifles, optics, ammo, etc. Folks, there are so many outstanding rifle, bow and optics suppliers on the market, there is absolutely no way that I would want to jump into that briar patch. Here is my response. 1) Determine a realistic budget that will not require you to sleep in the yard with the dog for spending too much money on hunting gear. 2) If possible try out every model that you are considering. Take into account the features, materials and performance that will make a difference to you personally. 3) Bring it home and begin using it to dial it in. 4) Do not settle for mediocre.

Personally, whether I am dialing in a new bow, crossbow or rifle, my goal is to consistently have a majority of my shots touching each other before hunting season comes around. You may say, you have got to be kidding me. No I am not. Twenty some odd years ago I hunted with a good buddy from Arkansas named Phil Weaver. At the time I thought Phil was a bit nuts about his compulsion to shoot a 5/8 inch group at 100 yards with his trusty elk rifle. I mean Phil would just not let up on it. After awhile I just started tuning him out as I could not see the point of worrying about that level of detail in my shooting. What I learned from Phil over the years was that Phil adhered to "aim small miss small." This translates to small errors at close range with your rifle or bow can translate in to much larger errors as range increases. Additionally, elk do not always provide the elk hunter with perfect broadside shots on level ground and good rests are sometimes hard to come by. Therefore, if our familiarity with our weapon and our level of practice at the range produces that 5/8" group, we are far better suited for the less than ideal shot offered in the field.

Recently I was at the range to familiarize myself with a new rifle, a Remington R-25 G2 MSR or Modern Sporting Rifle to be exact. These new hunting rifles are designed around the technology that originally gave our military the M16 and then the M4 carbine. MSRs are semi-auto and clip fed which is very different from the straight forward bolt guns that I have hunted with for most of my life. Prior to going to the range for the first time I did my homework by reading the owner's manual and watching videos on the operations of the weapon. I was paying particular attention to how to handle malfunctions with this new type of weapon. For those of you have served our country in the infantry of our

96

armed forces thank you for your service, but please cut me some slack as you read this. I flew in the Air Force. My entire exposure to these types of weapons was one familiarization and qualification course 35 years ago. Since that time, I have had little opportunity to train with or fire an MSR.

So when I squeezed the trigger for the first time....nothing. Ok, I'm good. I feel pretty sure that I know the procedure for safely handling and clearing a misfire. After going through the entire process of attempting to clear the weapon after a perceived misfire, I was still stuck with a hot weapon that I could not clear. With no other option, I swallowed my pride and called the range safety guy over to tell him of the problem. He too tried all the same procedures as I had tried with the same result. He says, let me get another guy. In less than a minute along comes range safety guy #2 who appears to be a in his mid-twenties. He too works through exactly the same process with the same result that both range guy #1 and I had tried. It was then that this professional's intimate knowledge of the weapon saved the day so to speak. After insuring that all was safe, he points the barrel skyward and gives the butt stock a swift pop onto the elevated table top, causing the jammed bolt to release and out pops the hung up round. Problem solved. He knew the details of the weapon intimately and it was this level of knowledge that made the difference. It is the level of detail that we as safe and ethical elk hunters need to have regarding our weapons of choice. He was a master of the weapon.

## The Killing Rock

If you are in your twenties or thirties and in the peak of physical health willing to go as far as it takes to harvest your bull...just skip over this section. I'm writing this brief passage on what has come to be known as the Killing Rock for hunters who, for whatever reason, are unable to

97

hump all day in pursuit of elk, but are unwilling to surrender their seat around the fire at elk camp. To these valiant "never give up" souls...well done good and faithful servant! Consider the Killing Rock.

I first heard the term Killing Rock from a long time outfitter in central Colorado who I'll call Jim. Jim shared with me that every season he would have a least one client who just wasn't up to day long hikes of miles and miles into the backcountry. Yet they were willing to pay him thousands of dollars for an elk hunt. As it happened, Jim had this stand located not too far from camp near a well used elk travel corridor. As Jim put it, there was no way to predict what time elk would use this game trail that passed near the stand, but it was clear that it was well used. Jim's theory was that if a hunter sat on that stand long enough, he might get a chance shot without having to walk too far. The key was motivating the hunter to sit still all day for as many days as it took. While there were no guarantees that this hunter would even see an elk, most were willing to give it a try. It would appear that patience was one of the virtues that came with getting older. So every year a few of Jim's hunters would climb up on the "Killing Rock" and hunker in for the wait. And according to Jim about 30 percent of these hunters scored a bull. Not bad odds actually.

If you fit the bill, consider locating your own Killing Rock. Get yourself something to sit on. Bring along plenty of water, maybe a book and some snacks...and wait 'em out. You too may whack yourself a bull at your own personal Killing Rock.

# Navigating Elk Country: Map, Compass & GPS
**Paige Darden & My Topo Team**

*My sincere thanks to my longtime friend Paige Darden and her team of pros at MyTopo.com for their generous contribution to this chapter. These folks are the pros on land navigation tools. Whenever you are in need of almost anything to do with navigation, check them out at www.mytopo.com.*

Search and rescue professionals report that most of their missions focus on people on day trips, and 40% of those are hikers and hunters. Hunters who leave the trail in pursuit of game can become disoriented; push boundaries, often going further and staying out later than planned. Like anyone in the backcountry, they can experience medical emergencies that result in the need for rescue.

How do you avoid becoming one of those statistics? Plan ahead, carry and understand your map, sync your navigation tools, and stay found! In this chapter, you will learn how to use a map, compass and GPS together to ensure that you can navigate your way to hunting success as well as back to your truck!

99

To help you plan and strategize your hunt, there are a plethora of online maps, desktop mapping software and mobile apps available. Google Earth is a popular tool for research. MyTopo has a great free browsing service that allows you to switch between topo and aerial map layers to gain a better understanding of the land. Many navigation apps come with a desktop interface and/or you can purchase a subscription to a mapping service that includes editing tools. Using these tools, you can mark key spots like trail heads, water sources, potential bedding areas, food sources, campsites, etc. If the service includes measuring tools, you can determine the distance between points. All of your marked waypoints can then be saved as a .GPX file to use in your Smartphone or GPS device. This information can also be emailed to your friends. A .gpx file is the most common file format to share location-based data. Most mapping programs and GPS devices can import/export .GPX files. If you use Google Earth, you will have to translate from Google's proprietary .KML file data to .GPX using one of several free KML to GPX conversion services available on the Internet.

Planning ahead also should involve printing maps. For multi-day trips, it is especially smart to use a service like MyTopo Map Pass ($29.95 a year) to print true-to-scale maps with your own annotations on them. These are formatted for desktop printing, allowing prints of the standard 8.5 x 11 or 11 x 17. Smart hunters will use editing tools to mark where they plan to park, camp on day 1, day 2, day 3, etc. These maps can be left in the truck, at the ranger station and with loved ones, and will be invaluable should the hunting party require rescue. Search and rescue folks report that they often have to spend two or more hours trying to find a hunters truck before they even begin the rescue mission. Oftentimes, the only information they have to go on is that the person was hunting in a particular mountain range or wildlife management area and didn't come home. That mountain range or

WMA can be huge with many places to enter and exit making a rescue attempt very challenging.

Every person should also carry a large-format, waterproof map with them. These can be ordered from MyTopo.com. MyTopo prints and ships every order within 24 hours, and the maps can be custom-centered to include the area of focus. Topographic maps and aerial/satellite imagery maps can also include public and private land boundaries, US Forest Service roads and trails, and Game Management Unit boundaries providing all of the critical information on one map sheet.

**Understanding Your Map**
Once you have your map, it is important to understand all of the data in the map legend. One of the first issues to check is the map scale. A common map scale is 1:24,000, the native scale of the United States Geological Survey 7.5 minute topographic map series, which are widely recognized as the most detailed maps available in the United States. A 1:24000 scale means one inch on the map is equal to 24,000 inches (2000 feet) on the ground. A hunter travelling 2 miles per hour on a straight, flat trail would cover roughly 5.3 inches on a 1:24,000 map. You can do this same type of calculation on any map, but you must first understand the map scale.

On topographic maps, contour lines indicate elevation change. The closer they are together, the steeper the terrain. Tightly packed lines indicate cliffs, and you should recognize them as a place to avoid when venturing off-trail. Of course, big game, like humans, also try to find the path of least resistance between their food and water resources and bedding areas. Understanding the topography of the land can help you to strategize your hunt.

On USGS topo maps, the contour interval varies from 5 feet to 40 feet. To determine the interval, look for the darker 'indicator' lines and count the number of lines between them. Somewhere along the indicator line you will find a number indicating the number of feet above sea level. You can subtract the lower number from the higher number, and divide by the number of contour lines between the indicator lines to derive at the contour interval. Summits are marked with triangles and hills and high areas are indicated by circles. There are hundreds of symbols indicating roads, trails, gravel pits, sand, water, and more. For a complete list of USGS symbols, refer to the official USGS symbol guide. Studying a topographic map with the USGS symbol guide handy can help you determine if the area has former mine sites, and all kinds of interesting tidbits of information that can be both useful and interesting.

**Public Land / Private Land Boundaries**
When hunting, it is solely the responsibility of the hunter to know whether he or she is legally allowed to be on the land. You can take it to the bank that the game warden will not accept "sorry, I didn't know" as an answer. In the West, there is a patchwork of ownership between the Bureau of Land Management, the US Forest Service, State-owned lands, National Parks, Native American Reservations and more. Each land is managed independently, with its own rules and regulations for hunting. A good hunting map will have public land ownership boundaries included, with a legend to explain who manages each section of land. It is a good idea to check with the local office that manages the land where you will be hunting to find out important up-to-date information such as whether there are any new road closures, bear activity, forest fire threat levels, and other always-changing information.

**True North vs. Magnetic North**

Now that you understand your printed map, it is important to sync your printed map with your GPS and compass. For your compass, the most important issue is the magnetic declination, or the difference between True North and Magnetic North, which is where your compass will point. In the legend or key of your map, you will find the declination, such as 11 degrees East depicted. I recommend that you use a declination adjustable compass, like the Brunton TruArc 10, that can be set to account for the declination. That way your compass will point to the same north as your paper map, and you will avoid having to adjust for declination every time you put your compass on your map. The red arrow on your compass will point north and you can position your map under the compass so that the map matches the real terrain around you. If you want to learn all about triangulation, headings and bearings for true map/compass navigation, take an orienteering class and do lots of practice. But, for the average hunter, simply knowing how to use a compass with your paper map as explained above is enough.

**GPS**

Today, most hunters carry a smart phone with them, and nearly every Smartphone comes with a GPS chip inside of it that is exactly the same technology used in standalone GPS devices. So, your Smart phone can serve as your GPS device, saving you a bundle of money. And, most people do not realize that the GPS technology in your phone is completely separate from the cellular network you use to make calls allowing your phone to be used as your GPS even when you are completely out-of-network. In fact, you will want to keep your phone in airplane mode to save battery power when using your phone as your GPS. To set up your phone as your GPS device, you will simply need to go to your app store and download a navigation app, like Viewranger, Backcountry GPS, Gaia, OnXMaps, or any number of others.

Whether you are using a standalone GPS or a smart phone with a navigation app, you need to make sure your GPS matches your printed map. The first step is the match the map datum. The most common formats are NAD27 (commonly seen on older maps) and WGS84/NAD83 (the most recent datum and the default setting for most maps and GPS devices in the United States.) Next you will need to match the coordinate system. The two most common are latitude/longitude or universal transverse Mercator (UTM). Under SETTINGS on your GPS/Smartphone app, you can change the settings to match those on your map.

Unfortunately, most GPS devices and apps do not come loaded with detailed maps for the entire US. You will need to install maps before you leave on your trip. For GPS units, you will need to purchase a memory card with maps which is usually sold separately. For Smartphone apps, most good apps have the option to "cache" or download maps for offline use.

> *Sidebar:* *If you are using your Smartphone and have a navigation app installed, you can swap .gpx files with friends who also have a Smartphone and navigation app. Simply email a .gpx file to your Smartphone. Open your email and press and hold on the attached .GPX file. Scroll to the GPS app installed on your phone and hit OK to import the GPS file into your mobile app. You can then view all the points, tracks and routes in the app. This is great way to share hunting plans with your buddies. You can also find many open source .GPX files available on the Internet. It is increasingly common for Departments of Natural Resources, BLM offices, US Forest Service offices and others to release data about road and trail networks in the .GPX file format. Remember, you can also upload the .GPX file to overlay*

*on your printed maps at MyTopo.com. And, if your navigation app has a desktop interface, you can view GPX files on the desktop and phone, sharing and syncing between your devices, as well as sharing with friends' devices.*

## UTM

Lastly, you should learn to use the UTM grid. It is very easy to learn and is the grid format used by the military, SAR teams and adventure racers for precise land navigation. It is easier than lat/long because it equally divides the land into one-kilometer grids on a 1:24,000 map. To learn how to use the UTM grid, visit www.maptools.com. There you will find videos, quizzes and helpful tips. There are also many YouTube videos that explain the UTM grid.

With the UTM grid on your printed map and as the setting in your GPS device, you can use your GPS and printed map hand-in-hand. The GPS device will give you the blue dot to show you your precise location, and you can then relate that coordinate reading to your printed map. Visa versa, you can see a point on your printed map, and log that point into your GPS device and then use the GO TO feature to have your GPS lead you to that place. Ideally, you will have digital maps that match your printed maps, making it that much easier to relate your GPS device reading to your printed map.

With these tips, you are set to navigate in the backcountry. Remember, plan your trip ahead of time; sync your compass, GPS, and printed map; and check your location frequently throughout your trip. Using your digital and printed maps together to make sure you know where you are, along with a compass to keep you pointed in the correct direction, and you will have great hunting success. You will also avoid tax payer dollars having to be used to rescue you, except in a medical emergency

Jay Houston

situation.  Even if you or someone in your party needs to be rescued, if you have followed the steps outlined, your rescue will be far less expensive and more likely to result in success.  There is no downside to using mapping tools and technology to strategize your hunts and navigate successfully. Today's tools make it easy for anyone to become a competent map reader and navigator.

**Staying Found**

Now that you have your printed map, your compass, and your GPS/Smartphone working properly together, you are almost ready to begin your adventure.  Here are a few tips to "stay found".  First, leave a detailed itinerary with your loved ones and local law enforcement, including leaving printed maps with your plan overlaid on the map, or emailing a .GPX file with your trip plan outlined.  When on your adventure, keep your map and your GPS handy, not stashed away in the bottom of your backpack.  This way you can follow your progress on the map, keeping a mental map of where you have been.  Always match key land features to the map such as trail junctions, creek, ridges, etc.  It is also important to keep track of time so you can match your pace with the map scale.   A good navigator will check their map every 15-30 minutes.

Jason Balaz, Colorado

## DRT Means Dead Right There

I appropriated this term from some of my brothers who served in Iraq and Afghanistan. DRT translates to **D**ead **R**ight **T**here. Though I think it is self explanatory, in the context of this discussion it means preparing to

107

make a shot that drops the bull right where he is standing. This assures a humane harvest negating the need for a lengthy search.

There are many factors that might come into play that could preclude the DRT result. Such factors include: wind drift, inaccurate range assessment, target motion, relative target angle, and a host of factors that can be attributed to the shooter himself. That being said, it is our responsibility as ethical elk hunters to make every possible effort in our preparation and at the time of the shot to assure a DRT outcome. Let's take a look at what an elk hunter can do to increase the odds of a DRT result focusing some tips on precision shoot for both rifle and bow.

*Our sincere thanks to John L. Plaster, Major, Special Forces, U.S. Army (ret) for his service to our country and for the following lesson on precision rifle shooting. To learn more, see his website at http://ultimatesniper.com.*

**Ten Components of Precision Rifle Shooting**
**John L. Plaster**

1. **Properly Mount, Focus and Zero Your Scope:** This is the foundation for accurate shooting. Incorrect eye relief precludes holding your rifle naturally with a proper cheek weld, while canting adds a degree of error that grows with distance. Zero your scope at exactly your intended distance -- usually 200 yards for elk -- and at least yearly re-focus your scope's reticle so it's crisp.

2. **Determine Your Most Accurate Load:** Before I zero, I typically fire four or five different loads to find the most accurate one for

that rifle. Accuracy differences can be profound, even among various match loads.

3. **Focus on Fundamentals:** Practice trigger control by "educating" your finger to that specific trigger, especially through dry firing. Perfect your sight picture -- the scope's entire field-of-view should be clear, with the crosshair centered. As your shot breaks, your eye is focused on the crosshair, not the target. For breath control take a couple of deep breaths to oxygenate your blood. Exhale normally. Then, on a half-breath, during your natural respiratory pause, break your shot -- that's when your body is calmest. After firing, pause for a second. Follow-through by continuing to look through your scope and breathe. Then immediately run your bolt. This helps maintain your mental focus right through the shot. The habit of running the bolt ensures that you always have a round ready for a follow-on shot.

4. **Record Each Shot:** Carefully record each shot in a Marksmanship Record Book. This teaches you to focus on each shot as a one-time event, which enables you to analyze any inaccuracy. Fire no more than ten rounds per paper target and "call" each shot -- that is, immediately after firing a shot, before eyeing the target, jot down where you THINK it impacted, then see exactly where it did impact and record it. Calling your shot will sensitize you to tiny errors as you break each shot.

Laser rangefinders are great -- but first estimate distances the old-fashioned way.

5. **Master Range Estimation:** The greatest cause of long-range misses is incorrect range estimation. This has a cumulative

impact when compensating for distance, wind, target movement and uphill/downhill angle. Fight the temptation to round-off or snap-judge a distance such as 350 yards. Instead, narrow it to the closest five yards. I have several lasers and use them often, but mostly as a "de-liar." -- That is, FIRST I estimate the range using a technique such as estimating half that distance and doubling it, or using football-field 100-yard increments. Only after that do I use a laser to determine how close my estimate was -- and if it was wrong, analyze how I went wrong.

6. **Learn to Estimate and Compensate for the Wind:** So-called "doping the wind" is a long-range shooter's greatest challenge because it's part skill and part art. The best way to learn it is to do it. Electronic wind gauges are helpful, but they only measure the wind at your location. -- I consider these devices a "yardstick" for comparing the wind around me to the wind downrange. Equally important, know how the wind affects your projectile and (as a starting point) memorize the amount of wind drift at various distances and from various angles.

7. **Understand and Employ Minute-of-Angle Measurements:** The basic increment of most American riflescopes is a fraction of a Minute-of-Angle, usually one-quarter of a Minute, which means one-quarter inch at 100 yards. Learn exactly what your scope's increments (or "clicks") equal, and how this increases with distance.

8. **Confirm the Trajectory of YOUR Rifle/Scope/Ammo Combination:** Through brochures or websites, obtain your ammo manufacturer's exterior ballistics for your load. Make special note of the trajectory which shows how much your bullet drops at various distances, after zeroing at 100 or 200

yards. This is useful data but it's not "gospel" because it assumes a 24-inch barrel, shooting at sea level, in 59 degrees F., with a scope mounted one and one-half inches over the bore. The combination of YOUR rifle, YOUR scope and YOUR ammo may vary the trajectory a bit, which can only be measured by actually firing at various distances. Jot down these variances (preferably fired at 25 yard increments) so you know EXACTLY where your bullet will impact.

Shooting off a bench at known distances is OK for zeroing, but practice fire requires unknown distances in field conditions -- prone, sitting, standing and kneeling.

9. **Practice-Fire on Shooting Ranges AND in Field Conditions:** Divide your live-fire practice between "Known Distance" firing from a bench or prone, and "Unknown Distance" firing in field conditions, which employs all body positions. I consider Known Distance firing only zero verification -- that is, it only confirms that my zero is correct and prepares me for realistic practice. Get off the shooting bench and practice the sitting, kneeling, squatting, prone and offhand positions. Firing at unknown distances integrates target detection, range estimation, body positions and marksmanship. I advocate shooting in inclement weather -- recall that Carlos Hathcock used to say, "It never rains on a rifle range." Keep it fun, using reactive targets such as clay pigeons, balloons and steel plates. And finally, I recommend focusing on "quality shots," rarely firing more than 20 rounds during a single practice session -- that way, each shot matters.

10. **Strive for Consistency:** Accuracy follows consistency. Be consistent in everything you do, from how you hold your rifle to how you see the scope sight picture, break the shot, breathe -- everything. Develop the consciousness to diagnose the source of any error, and then consistently apply the correction. The more consistently you operate, the more accurately you will shoot.

*The following is generously contributed by one of my best friends, fellow military aviator and hunting buddy Roger Medley, a nationally ranked archer and bowhunter; author and host of Backcountry Bowhunting.*

**Archery Accuracy**
**Roger Medley**

Many books, articles and blog posts have been written about archery accuracy. For the sake of space and time we'll focus on a few foundational areas.

**Bow Tuning & Arrow Aerodynamics:** Getting arrows to fly well has been a huge issue for many for a long time. This problem has launched a multi-million dollar business segment for mechanical (expandable) broadheads.

A number of years ago I was watching a well known bowhunting TV show. The host was spending some time with a shooting coach (a very wise thing for all of us to do.) When the TV host admitted that he screws in his broadheads. He would then re-sight in his bow. I was surprised. When switching from field points to broadheads and using the same weight point, the weight of the arrow doesn't change.

Therefore the arrow should fly that same. However, we've all experienced that they don't always fly that same. So, why is that? Actually, there's a very simple explanation. It's simple aerodynamics.

As a kid I would put my hand out of the window while we were driving down the road and "fly" my hand up and down. If I angled my hand up and then the airflow would take my hand higher. Angle my hand down, it would fly down.

Similarly, with a broadhead, especially a fixed blade, the blades are basically an extra set of vanes on the front of the arrow. If an arrow is leaving the bow slightly nose down (up or left or right) the arrow will fly even further in that direction. That explains why the "my broadheads don't fly like my field points". So why do field point's hit more consistently? Field points are aerodynamically forgiving, a broadhead is not.

Here is one way to improve your archery accuracy. Once your bow is sighted in to your maximum shooting distance, shoot a field point arrow and a broadhead arrow at 20 yards. Compare where the broadhead lands to where the field point lands. Keep doing this out to your maximum shooting distance as long as the broadhead arrow is still landing in the target.

If the broadhead arrow lands lower than your field point arrow, adjust the rest up a very slight amount, i.e. a 1/32nd of an inch. Repeat the shot. The concept is that we want to move the broadhead arrow to where the field point arrow is landing. Only very slight movement is usually needed. Three inches low at 60 yards means the rest should only be moved approximately 1/32nd of an inch up. Keep making the necessary adjustments until the field points and broadheads are landing together at all distances.

113

Jay Houston

**Shot Process:** I grew up around airplanes. When my father taught me to fly, he said that a good landing starts before you even get near the airport. His meaning was that a good landing starts well in advance of the landing itself, and is the result of a process or sequence of deliberate steps. It doesn't happen by accident.

Your shot process is similarly important? Sighting in your bow is priority one. Since a bow is a mechanical device it will perform consistently. However if you're not consistently doing your part how can you be sure your bow is actually sighted in accurately? An inconsistent grip in the bow hand can make a difference of several inches at 20 yards.

Keep your shot process the same regardless of the target. For hunting scenarios simply speed up the process. The more familiar you are with your process the more ingrained it will become and be natural to you.

Step 1 - Align yourself with the target. Your feet should be approximately shoulder width apart, align yourself with the target. Ensure that you're standing strong, straight and in a "T" shape with your shoulders square.

Step 2 - Nock your arrow. Ensure that your arrow is nocked properly. This means that the nock is in the correct position and the bow string is fully engaged into the nock. I've found it helpful to use the indexing tab on the side of nock as a reference point. If need be, I can nock my arrow without even looking by simply feeling the indexing tab.

Step 3 - Establish your grip. Another thing my father taught me about flying is that a death grip on the control wheel will prevent you from feeling the subtle things that are happening with the plane. A light touch is all that is needed. The same holds true for your bow. A very light grip is all that is needed.

Step 4 - Choose your impact point. Be specific. I was the pitcher for my little league baseball team, but I was never taught how to pitch. The coach simply said *"look hard at where you want the ball to go and throw it there"*. If it's the upper left spot on a target or a tuft of hair behind the shoulder of a 400 class bull elk, choose your impact point and focus there – be specific.

Step 5 - Raise your bow with your bow arm fully extended. Once your bow is on target, begin the next step of drawing your bow.

Step 6 - Draw your bow. Take 2 deep breaths before drawing your bow. This will give your muscles oxygen to work with.

Step 7 - Anchor point. A good anchor point is made up of 3 points.

1. Where your hand or knuckle rests against your ear or cheek.
2. The tip on your nose should touch the string.
3. Align your round site pin guard in the center of your peep site.

Step 8 - Level the bow. Use a sight with a level! A shot made with ½ of the bubble being outside of the lines can cause an arrow to impact left or right by as much as eight inches at 60 yards. It really is that important!

Step 9 - Allow the pin to float. You must be completely fine with letting the pin float over your impact point. If not, this is where "drive-by" shootings, also known as target panic, can take place. There is an urge to send the arrow on its way the next time the pin gets near the target.

An underlying cause is related to reduced muscle endurance or fatigue. For many this target panic gets worse the longer they hold, or try to hold, the pin on the target. As the muscles become drained of strength it becomes increasingly difficult to hold the pin on target. As the pin moves more and more the urge becomes greater to slap or "punch" the release trigger the next time the pin gets near the bull's-eye.

Step 10 - Breath Control. Taking two deep breaths prior to drawing your bow will give your muscles fresh oxygen to work with during the most critical part of the shot. One more deep breath after drawing the bow will give you strength to aim.

Step 11 - Aiming "Aim small" or aiming at a small specific spot will focus all your attention on aiming. Your mind shouldn't be on trigger control at this point – it should be on aiming. This is where a release with a light trigger pressure can be a real detriment to your accuracy. Your attention will be on your trigger finger and not on aiming. Making sure your finger doesn't touch the release and inadvertently send the arrow down range prematurely is a distraction.

A release with a heavy trigger pressure and little trigger travel is ideal. I've found that the Carter Enterprises Two Shot with a heavy spring (4 lbs of trigger pull) or the Carter Quickie are solid release platforms.

Step 12 - Increase Trigger Pressure. Continue to increase pressure on the trigger until the shot explodes.

Step 13 - Follow through. Eyes remain on target.

**Kevin Fair, Colorado**

# Size Matters: Finding and Killing Trophy Bulls

Before we start down this path, we need to pause to consider the question, what constitutes a trophy?

> The term trophy has its origins in the Latin referring to a
> memorial of an ancient Greek or Roman victory raised on the
> field of battle, or a representation of such a memorial inscribed

117

on perhaps a medal; something gained or given in victory or conquest especially when preserved or mounted as a memorial.
~Merriam-Webster Dictionary

I especially like that last one...mounted as a memorial. So how big does a trophy bull elk have to be in order achieve 'over the mantel' status? 260, 300, 360, 400 or more.

Over the years I have seen my share of wall hangers and to tell you the honest truth, there have been more of these trophies **UNDER** the elusive 300-inches than over. But, without exception, when the owner of the trophy shows it to you, there is always a smile on their face and a true sense of accomplishment in their eyes. The old saying is true, "beauty is in the eye of the beholder." Let's take a look at what some notables in the industry have to say about what constitutes a record bull.

**The Boone and Crockett Club**

Known for its strict adherence to a Fair Chase doctrine, the Boone and Crockett Club has, since its founding in 1887 by Theodore Roosevelt, been recognized as a leader in issues that affect hunting, wildlife and wild habitat. The Boone and Crockett Club promotes selective hunting for mature big game species as a game management tool for maintaining balanced and healthy herd populations. The Club's North American Big Game records program serves as a vital conservation record for documenting the success of wildlife management programs.

> The scoring system depends upon carefully taken measurements of the enduring trophy characteristics to arrive at a numerical final score that provides instant ranking for all trophies of a category. By measuring only enduring characters

118

(such as antlers, horns, and skulls) rather than skin length or carcass weight, the measurements may be repeated at any later date to verify both the measurements and the resulting ranking in each category. The system places heavy emphasis on symmetry, penalizing those portions of the measured material that are non-symmetrical. This results in even, well-matched trophies scoring better and placing higher in the rankings than equally developed but mismatched trophies, a result that most people readily agree with and accept. For those antlered trophies with unusual amounts of abnormal antler material, non-typical categories were developed to give them recognition, as they would be unduly penalized in the typical categories.

Trophies that meet the Awards minimum but not the All-Time minimum will be listed in the Awards book. Trophies that meet the All-Time minimum will be listed in both the Awards book, as well as "Records of North American Big Game." [1]

**Minimum B&C Entry Scores:**

|  | Awards | All-Time |
|---|---|---|
| American Typical Elk | 360 | 375 |
| American Non-Typical Elk | 385 | 385 |
| Tule Elk | 270 | 285 |
| Roosevelt's Elk | 275 | 290 |

**Pope and Young Club**
Founded in 1961 and modeled after the Boone and Crockett Club, the Pope and Young Club advocates and encourages responsible bowhunting by promoting quality, fair chase hunting, and sound conservation practices. Via its Records Program, the Pope and Young Club encourages excellence in bowhunting by arousing awareness and promoting exceptional examples of American big game. The Club records information on North American big game taken with bow and arrow.[2]

**Minimum P&Y Entry Scores:**

| | |
|---|---|
| American Typical Elk | 260 |
| American Non-Typical Elk | 335 |
| Roosevelt's Elk | 225 |

**Safari Club International**
Safari Club International Foundation (SCIF) is a non-profit charitable organization that funds and manages worldwide programs dedicated to wildlife conservation, outdoor education and humanitarian services. SCI provides value to its members by shaping policies and legislation that protect the freedom to hunt.

**Minimum SCI Entry Scores:**

|  | Min. General | Min. Archery |
|---|---|---|
| Rocky Mtn. Typical Elk | 265 | 235 |
| Rocky Mtn. Non-Typical Elk | 278 | 247 |
| Roosevelt's Elk | 245 | 225 |
| Tule Elk | 245 | 220 |

For the purposes of this discussion I am going to use 300 B&C as a baseline when referring to trophy bulls. For nearly 20 years of working with clients looking for a trophy elk hunt, better than the 300-point threshold is what most indicate they are talking about when asked to define what the word trophy means to them. Every western elk state holds a share of these 300-class or better bulls. Some states hold far more than others. But for most hunters the big question is how do we plan a hunt for a trophy bull? (By the way, if you were hoping that I would tell you exactly where to find a trophy bull that is not going to happen here.) What I am going to do is give you some good tips that will help you get your homework moving in the right direction. Those who take the time to invest themselves in the preparation, more often than not reap greater rewards.

**Search the Record Books**
If you are really looking for an area that will produce a bull that will get your name in the record books, go directly to the source. All three of the above mentioned organizations track the information on where bulls

entered into their record book were taken. Usually the entry will have a reference to a city, town, or county in the particular state where it was taken. It will also usually indicate the year (if available) in which the animal was harvested. A few hours of research will start to give you a picture of which states and which areas within that state produce the bigger bulls.

**Outfitters Association's Best of Species Awards**
Some states have Outfitter Associations that track trophy harvests of their member outfitters. Each year the association awards something similar to a "Best of Species" award to the outfitter who brings in the biggest bull. In many states you will see the name of the same outfitter popping up year after year. It is then just a matter of finding out which area(s) that outfitter hunts to narrow down your search for an area that produces bigger or trophy class bulls. If the outfitter hunts on the National Forest or BLM land, the US Forest Service or BLM maintains this information respectively.

**State by State Breakout for Trophy Bulls**

**Arizona**: If you're looking to set a new world record, Arizona offers some of the best opportunities for 400-class or better bulls and the South Kaibab may be at the top of the list. While drawing one of the coveted tags in this area with low hunting pressure and strong genetics is extraordinary, it is not impossible. Some of the best public land opportunities for trophy bulls can be found in units 9 and 10. Other areas producing B&C bulls include units: 4A, 5A&B, 6A&B, 7 and 8. For those who can afford the price tag, the San Carlos Apache reservation may offer the best genetics in the state. If you are not in a position to

122

pay top dollar, look closely at the public land surrounding the reservation.

**New Mexico**: 320 to 330-class bulls can be found regularly in Units 16A-E, 21A and 21B of New Mexico's Gila National Forest, and bulls exceeding 350 are not all that uncommon for the hunter who is willing to put some miles on his boots in this Piñon-Juniper covered wilderness. Other areas with good trophy potential include units 4, 10, 12, 13 and 55. For those able to afford the price of admission, The Mescalero Apache Reservation usually produces at least one 400-class monster each year. A more affordable hunt can usually be found on the Jicarilla Apache Reservation. While you will likely see 350 or better bulls there, you probably won't encounter anything approaching the 400-class bulls found on the Mescalero Apache Reservation. Keep in mind that all elk tags (except land owner tags) in New Mexico are obtained via a lottery and it may take years of applying before you draw. The strategy for hunting states that only offer tags via a draw system is to begin putting in for as many of these states as you can. Have a backup plan for hunting one of the states offering over-the-counter tags such as Colorado or Idaho until you draw.

**Utah**: If you're planning on hunting one of Utah's premium limited-entry areas be prepared to part with some cash. 2016 premium limited entry non-resident elk tags run $1505. Though not a state typically know for record elk harvests, Utah has produced most of the biggest bulls in recent years. Areas to consider if you're planning a big bull hunt in Utah include: Book Cliffs, North Slope-Three Corners, North Slope-Summit and West Daggett, Box Elder-Grouse Creek and Box Elder-Pilot Mountain.

Jay Houston

**Colorado**: While Colorado hosts the largest elk herd in the US numbering in excess of 300,000 (2016), it is known as the elk hunting capital of the world for turning out the largest elk harvest annually. However it is not necessarily known for delivering large numbers of trophy class bulls as compared to other states. This does not mean that Colorado does not produce a respectable share of 300-class or better bulls each year. For the public land hunter GMU 76 offers excellent opportunities for larger bulls. Just west of Montrose GMU 62 is also another favorite. GMU's 86 and 861 in the southern Sangre de Cristo are other destinations for those seeking trophy class bulls, but be prepared to pay to hunt private land or do a backpack type hunt as the access to public land is limited and the terrain can be brutal. Farther north GMU 14 in the Mt. Zirkel Wilderness usually produces some really nice bulls as well. Keep in mind that hunting areas designated as wilderness means you will be limited to foot or horseback travel as there are no motorized vehicles allowed in these areas. Also look to the Gore Range at the higher elevations. Lower elevations on public land are heavily hunted forcing more mature bulls to hide out as high as they can get.

One of the best-kept secrets for bigger bulls in Colorado is private ranches (fair chase hunting) that consistently hold trophy 320 to 385-class bulls and are located east of I-25 in the southern Colorado Piñon-Juniper mesas. To look at these ranches you would never guess that they hold elk, but looks can be deceiving. While these are few and far between, for prices not too far above those of public land guided hunts, a smart hunter has an excellent chance of scoring on the bull of a lifetime. 2016 pricing is in the $8500 range which is a steal for trophy action on 340+ class bulls. One particular ranch that I know of boasts a

124

bull to cow ratio of 100:100 and will not allow hunters to take bulls less than 320 B&C.

**Nevada:**  If you are fortunate enough to draw a tag, Nevada offers some of the best opportunities for coming home with a huge trophy bull. For example, in recent years almost 70% of the bulls taken carried 6-point or better racks. If you want to focus on really large Nevada bulls look to units 111-115 around Ely. The genetics throughout Nevada are good, but those found around Ely are truly exceptional. If you are looking to draw a tag, be prepared for what could possibly be a very long wait. Nevada does offer landowner tags but they are some of the priciest in the West.

**Wyoming**: If you're looking for bigger bulls in Wyoming a number of destinations come to mind. First is the area surrounding the National Elk Refuse in Jackson Hole. While hunting on the refuge is not allowed, there are a number of migration routes leading to it where a strategically placed hunter might do well, particularly in the Gros Ventre range. You also might want to consider east of Yellowstone National Park in the Thorofare Wilderness.

**Montana**: Areas around Yellowstone, Glacier National Parks and along the Idaho-Montana border produce some extremely nice bulls. Due to the ruggedness of this terrain hunting pressure is relatively light. If you like straight up and straight down, this is the area for you. Bulls on both sides of the border seem to achieve the desired 6x6 racks somewhat earlier than bulls in the eastern part of the state.

**Idaho**: For whatever reason, Idaho seems to have remained a well-kept secret as a haven for bigger bulls. This may be due to the difficulty in navigating the terrain in much of the state. If there is one word to describe elk hunting in Idaho it is...tough. Few are those who are willing to make the effort required to get on these big Idaho bulls. Areas to consider include: the Salmon River drainage, Teton, Kootenai, Shoshone, and Fremont counties. In addition to Colorado it is also one of the few remaining states where over-the-counter tags are still available.

If you're looking to hook up with a trophy class bull on public land, you need to be mentally and physically prepared to do whatever it takes and go wherever you have to in order to find them. You need to get smart on why elk do what they do. For the average elk hunter looking to score on any legal bull, 80% of the effort will be in finding the elk. When you narrow your search down to that small group of bulls that have survived at least five hunting seasons or more, locating that special bull becomes about 98% of your effort.

Remember there is only a marginal chance of bumping into a 300-class or better bull anywhere near areas that are frequented by other hunters. Drainage heads with succulent grasses, moist valley floors, timbered transition areas, the bottom of the ugliest hole you can find; these are places in which to start your search. If you are considering a stand, ask yourself:

1. Does it overlook a well used food or water source?
2. Does it offer security?
3. Is it on or near a transition route?
4. Is it far...far away from other hunters?
5. Is there an elk standing in the middle of it?

If yes is not the answer to at least one of the above, consider another location.

*You will never experience excellence as long as you settle for mediocre. ~JH*

## Understanding Elk Behavior is Critical

**Bugling**

Not too long ago I was bowhunting a steep brushy slope in Northern Idaho when out of nowhere and without the least bit of warning my hunting partner and I were enveloped by what I can only describe as a raspy guttural roaring from somewhere really close by. As the sheer volume of sound echoed about the forest around me the hairs on the back of my neck literally stood straight up. I instinctively dropped to one

128

knee in some sort of prehistoric hunter's defensive posture wondering what was about to run over me. In mere seconds my body was flooded with about a gallon and a half of adrenaline and my fight or flight mechanism came to full alert. In that part of the state the cover is so dense that in the course of five days of hunting, I had no less than four similar up close and personal encounters with bulls screaming their heads off at me, yet I only saw one.

The typical mature elk bugle frequently consists of three parts, though this is not always the case. The bugle begins with a low sometimes raspy sound emanating from deep in the bull's gut. It then gradually rises to a high-pitched scream, which can quickly span as many as three octaves, often holding the highest note before promptly falling off quickly to another low frequency series of grunts or chuckles.

Here is a mental picture that some of us may remember, that I hope will give you an idea of what I'm trying to describe. This is going to date me...so please keep the laughter to a minimum. Think of a bull's bugle as dropping the clutch (the bugle begins) on your 1969 three-speed Camero RS at a stoplight expecting to hear tires squealing and rubber burning. To your dismay you discover that you have the car in 2$^{nd}$ gear and not 1$^{st}$ gear. What happens...all 350 horsepower is now trying its best to escape, but the transmission will not let it. Slowly, yet in ever increasing increments (the bugle begins to shift into a higher frequency as more air is released) the Camero begins to move forward, faster and faster as the transmission catches up and releases all the energy that was trying to get loose. Now you shift into third gear (bugle octaves change) and the car zooms ahead achieving full release of the power within. The car is now at full bore (the peak of the bugle), then...with little warning all energy falls off, the engine gets quiet and then like an

129

afterthought it utters a few coughs...Uhug...Uhug...then silence again (the grunt and then the bugle ends). Remember...you're a sixteen-year-old kid and guess what...you're out of gas again!

A quick review of Physics 101 tells us that sound propagation is not as much a function of volume as it is of frequency. While volume (energy output) is a factor, it is the frequency of the sound that determines how far and through how much cover the sound can travel without distortion. High frequency sounds like those in the second part or scream of an elk bugle travel relatively short distances even though they are powered by a greater volume of air. While lower frequency sounds like those in the early stages of a bugle or the ending chuckle will actually carry for longer distances. Proof of this is evidenced by the US Navy's use of ELF or Extra Low Frequency sound for communication to its submarines that may be submerged and on patrol thousands of miles away from the source.

Bugling is first and foremost a means of advertisement to cows and bulls alike, and not as a challenge to fight to every bull in the valley, as many elk hunters believe. According to one of the most renowned elk researchers of all time, Valerius Geist, bulls bugle in an attempt to out advertise one another. It is the method bulls use to attract cows to them for the purpose of reproduction. When necessary, bulls bugle to make their claim on the cows in their harem known to other interloper bulls that may be nosing around the periphery of the herd.

Bulls also bugle during the mating ritual. Since it is the cow who determines with which bull and when she will mate; bulls that make unwanted sexual advances to a cow that is not ready are often met with...well, rejection, i.e. the cow just walks off in a submissive posture. This rejection often causes the bull to emit a shortened version of its bugle, perhaps as some vocal signal of its frustration. On the flip side, when bulls successfully mount a cow that is ready to mate, the act is violently quick and typically ends with the bull jumping clear off the ground followed by a bugle. Go figure....

## Urine Spraying

If much of the behavior elk exhibit during the rut is about advertisement, then I would be remiss if I failed to spend a few minutes talking about urine spraying. That's right, bull elk peeing all over themselves. No one ever said bull elk were much into personal hygiene and this definitely helps to make the argument. In reality urine spraying plays a vital role during the rutting ritual as another way that bulls advertise.

One late September my wife, Rae Ann and I were attending Elk Fest in Estes Park, Colorado. Our work day had come to an end so we decided to take a tour around town to see if we could get some pictures of any of the hundreds of elk that can usually be found wandering through town during that time of the year. I know, this doesn't sound like much of a hunting story. It's an elk behavior story and you observe elk behavior wherever the elk happen to be. This particular story took place on the Estes Park city golf course. When we arrived at the golf course, we found about two hundred elk herded up into roughly four small groups grazing on some really nice Bermuda grass that made up one of the courses fairways. Each group was under the watchful eye of a dominant or herd bull, with anywhere from two to four satellite bulls drifting around the edge of each of the smaller groups presumably looking for an opportunity to sneak in and breed one of the cows.

131

The herd bulls were doing a first rate job running back and forth from one end of their respective harem to the other chasing off raghorn after raghorn. All the while they were bugling at the top of their lungs to let the cows as well as the raghorns know who was in charge. This was clearly, a form of advertisement as we saw no challenges to these brutes in the course of about two hours of observation.

As we continued to watch one particular herd, I noticed that there was a nice 5x5 satellite bull that was starting to show some more aggressive behavior than the others. In one instance, this particular bull decided that he had enough of these two-legged creatures (people) encroaching on what he must have considered his territory. He promptly chased about three of them over a fence. Actually, it was pretty comical; one minute these tourists were snapping away with their digital cameras without a care in the world, although some are within twenty yards of a pretty worked up bull. Then all I could see were flip-flops and backsides flying over the fence. I thought I was going to split something I laughed so hard.

After running off the two-legged competition this bull must have been thinking pretty highly of himself as he began to spray. Spraying can take a number of forms from a light mist to a semi-directed stream, to a very heavy conical spray. The urine in most cases is directed at nearly right angles to the erected penis. Lowering his head almost to the ground, the bull began in the semi-directed stream mode by spraying his face briefly then moving rearward to spray the heavy mane under his neck. He worked this area over for a good minute. All the while, the bull is palpitating. Palpitation is a rhythmic throbbing of the light colored area behind the penis and can be easily seen as it bobs during the spraying.

132

Jay Houston

Occasionally, it would seem as if this particular bull would lose control of his aim as the urine stream would fire off to the left or right pretty much hosing down anything within four or five feet. Fortunately, all the folks in colorful shorts and flip-flops were well out of range by the time he started spraying. Once the bull had exhausted what I thought must have been a gallon or more, the spraying ceased and the bull knelt down and began to rub and roll around in the overspray that had fallen on the ground...presumably to make sure that nothing went to waste. Actually, the urine soaked ground had muddied up pretty good and made for a fine yet small wallow. Often bulls will follow up this behavior by rubbing their recently soaked neck mane and the preorbital glands below their eyes on a nearby tree. This leaves some of the urine soaked mud that they picked up in the wallow as another form of territorial advertisement.

Jay Houston

Checking Cows

**Herding and Harem Defense**

The rut is a time of competition, collection, advertisement, and dominance. Cows seek out dominant bulls as a way of narrowing the field and assuring themselves that they have access to the best genetics for reproduction. Bulls are continually advertising to attract cows to themselves, conditioning the cows to remain nearby, and when necessary herding the cows to keep them from straying.

I recently observed two groups of cows each accompanied by a herd bull. Both groups were feeding on opposite sides of a small creek. If I had to estimate, I would guess that the groups were about two hundred yards apart yet the creek seemed to act as a physical barrier keeping the groups from mingling.  For the better part of an hour, the cows were

Jay Houston

content to remain in their respective groups. Each bull was on full-time guard duty bugling and running from one end of his harem to the other as he consoled his cows, while keeping them nearby, and running off the younger satellite bulls that would from time to time attempt to make a run at one of the ladies. The bulls appeared to be equally matched in the five-year age range, one a nice 6x6 and the other a 6x7. Either of these bulls would have made a grand addition to any elk hunter's wall. Unfortunately, for me my hunting season was already complete, and I was remanded to the sidelines with only a camera.

As I observed the two groups I wondered what would happen if a few of these cows decided to cross the creek to the other bull. It was not long before I got my answer. A single cow dropped down into the creek and made her way over to the herd on the opposite side. I watched the two bulls to see what their respective reactions would be. While the gaining bull (bull #1) didn't seem to take much notice, the loosing bull (bull #2) that had been at the far end of the herd was getting pretty worked up. Regrettably for him there were two raghorns flirting around his end of the herd and he couldn't risk responding to the cow's departure with anything other than a parting "please come back sweetheart" bugle. I continued to watch the bull #1 on the opposite bank to see if there would be any sign of victory when I observed a second collared cow and her yearling calf start to make their way down into the creek about five minutes after the first. As she climbed the opposite bank, I guess her former boyfriend, bull #2, noticed her and this was about all he could take. Even though he appeared to be outweighed by the darker bull on the opposite side of the creek by at least a hundred pounds, bull #2 let out a husky roar and charged down the meadow about 75 yards and across the creek. I said to myself, this is going to be good as I waited for the battle to begin.

Bull #2 ran directly into the center of the cows on the opposite bank, stretched his neck and began to bugle and palpitate. Two things happened. The few cows that had scattered when he ran into the harem began to settle down and return to the group, and the larger darker bull #1 immediately trotted away about three hundred yards in complete submission. Clearly bull #2 even with lesser body size was able to make up the difference using a more assertive dominance display. Within ten minutes, with bull #1 now grazing farther down the meadow alone in defeat, the rest of bull #2s harem moved across the stream to join with the newly acquired harem to form a single group of about fifty cows.

Whenever one of the cows would begin to drift away, the new herd bull would lower his head below his shoulders and toss his antlers rearward along his back while moving towards the offending cow at an angle with his eyes averted often making a few grunts to console and encourage the cow to move back towards the herd. If the wayward cow failed to comply with this form of gentle persuasion, the bull would bring his antlers forward and make mock charges at the cow as a further enticement to get back in line. On a few occasions, I have actually witnessed bulls rush the cow and even horn them if their response was not want the bull wanted. Many times once the cow started to move back toward the herd, the bull would turn away from the cow and bugle. Since cows are really running the show, this bugle is more symbolic of the bull recognizing and acknowledging the cow's decision to submit and return to the herd.

Contrary to herding, bulls intent on mating with a particular cow will usually approach the cow from a more head on direction with his

136

antlers fully erect. This communicates to the cow that his intent is other than merely herding. A cow that shows interest will allow the bull to move around behind her where he will begin licking her to determine if she has come into season yet. If the cow is not yet ready or decides that this bull is not the guy she wants to dance with after all, she will usually move away displaying a sign of submission. If she determines that the bull is 'the guy,' she will assume a rear leg spread haunch low posture. Many times you can actually see the cows rear legs begin to quiver as she prepares for the bull.

This brief discussion is offered to demonstrate that while herding prior to mating; the bull's attention is predominantly focused on acquiring and holding cows. The advantage to the hunter who is aware of this period of diverted attention should be clear. He should use this to his advantage by creating a plan to close for the shot, especially if bowhunting. It is critical to keep in mind however that while the bull's attention may be diverted, he is surrounded by perhaps dozens of sets of eyes (cows) that are continually looking for other prospective mates and predators as well.

Your challenge is to close to within effective shooting range without alerting the cows. Here you have to keep a keen eye on the wind. As cows are continually moving about the periphery of the herd, a smart hunter can use his cow call making soft comforting mews to cover unexpected footfalls as he moves in. If you pay close attention to the wind and use cover, you would be better to move in with no sound at all as any sound can attract attention regardless of how well you call. The less attention you can draw to yourself, the better off you will be. Keep in mind that when stalking bulls that are herding cows, your real challenge is to beat the cows' defense mechanism.

137

Jay Houston

## Elk Travel Patterns

As we discussed earlier, elk spend roughly ninety percent of their time, the exception being the rut, eating and resting. So how do they spend the remaining three to four hours of any twenty-four hour period? The areas in which elk feed throughout early to mid fall (hunting season) and the habitat in which they lay up during the day to digest can be separated by significant distances, often miles. The smart hunter is one who takes the time to study and understand how elk transition from one area to the other, and the factors that may play into why the elk use these specific routes. He stands a far greater chance at scoring on an elk than the hunter who randomly traverses elk country taking his rifle or bow for an extended walk.

Keeping in mind our previous discussion on the Law of Least Effort, elk will use the same established trails year after year. Old travel routes usually found on timbered north or east facing slopes provide not only security but also make for ease of travel. For travel between drainages, elk like to use saddles, often not approaching them straight on which requires a lot more effort, but by using existing trails that run nearly parallel but just below the ridge top so as not to highlight themselves. If the saddle is open or exposed, the elk may move left or right for cover soon after crossing the ridge. If there is open territory on the far side of the saddle with little cover, elk may pause or slow for a minute to make sure that the coast is clear before entering a meadow. If cover is available within the saddle itself, elk will almost always remain in the cover. In either case, placing a stand or setting up just over the saddle may give you an opportunity for a shot at a stationary or slow moving elk.

Elk have been known to use old stock trails in areas that are subject to summer grazing by cattle once the cattle have been moved out of the area to lower pasture. If you happen to come across a well-used stock trail, look closely for signs of elk usage as well. I can't tell you how many times I have missed elk sign because I failed to look for it. I had mentally written off the trail because I thought only cattle or sheep were using it.

## Slopes

Though steep by human standards, slopes of ten to thirty percent are little challenge to elk for grazing or travel. I remember glassing a herd of elk in south central Colorado some years back on a scouting trip in late July. Though daytime temperatures were reaching into the seventies, there was still plenty of snow pockets trapped on the northern slopes above 11,000 feet. The elk were scattered over a quarter-mile of this particular slope which in some places appeared to be as much as a forty percent grade. All the while, they were feeding and staying cool lying in the snow as if they were on level ground. Research indicates that beyond about thirty percent, elk use usually drops off significantly, with little elk activity on slopes above fifty percent. The same research shows that elk use tends to increase with an increase in slope with the highest frequency of use found on slopes in the fifteen to thirty percent range. Had we tried to make our way up the slope to the elevation where the elk were, I seriously believe our lungs would have burst; for the elk, it was just routine. The argument here is that just because the slope is tough on the hunter does not mean that you won't find elk there.

During early fall when temps may still spike into the high seventies, elk frequently use creek and drainage bottoms for travel routes due to the promise of water, high quality forage, and thermal cover from the heat. Though difficult for the hunter to traverse because of the extreme

139

density of cover found bordering such areas, hunters should not dismiss these travel routes. Look for stands where you can observe these corridors especially where they may open up near the head of drainage. Also look for well used trails emerging from dark timber that feed into these creek bottoms. In areas where you can actually find moving water, look for elk sign in the cutbacks in the creek where water pools and elk may come to drink remaining under the cover of brush bordering the creek. While I am not a huge advocate of the use of tree stands for elk hunting, if you find a water source that is being frequented by elk, it could make for an excellent location to consider putting up a stand.

**Learning About Land & Travel Patterns from the Air**
Having spent an entire career flying in the Air Force and Air National Guard, I have acquired a keen sense of the perspective you gain from looking over an area from altitude. While it is not for everyone, if you have the resources, it's really not that expensive to take the opportunity to spend even a small amount of time over flying the area that you plan to hunt. You will learn more about that area and the general travel patterns of elk in one hour flying over the area than you will in a month of scouting on the ground. I am not saying that flying over your hunting area is a replacement for quality time spent scouting on the ground, but the bird's eye view from the air will provide you with information and a perspective that you will never get on the ground.

From the air, you will gain an acute sense of the typography of the land that perhaps 1% of hunters can discern from a topo map. If you have a topo of the area with you in the aircraft, what you see will help to clarify what the map is telling you. Make sure to take your GPS along on the flight to mark spots that may be of interest once you actually get on the

140

ground and begin hunting. In addition to learning how to access specific areas that you may want to hunt, the well used trails that elk leave in the open areas stand out clearly. In many cases you will see numerous trails paralleling one another across a slope indicating travel patterns. You will be able to see where these trails lead into dark timbered areas and where they come out on the opposite side. You will see which saddles are getting heavier use. Don't worry about seeing elk. That is not the objective. The over flight is to help you learn more about the area itself. If you do happen to see elk, well that's just icing on the cake.

Once the shooting begins elk tend to head to areas that are difficult for hunters to access. From the air, say 3,000-5,000 feet AGL (above the surrounding terrain) you will be able to look down into the bottom of some of those deep holes and cuts that you would in all likelihood never investigate, thus possibly missing out on a first-class elk area. If you plan to do some flying over elk country, make sure to check out the local laws in this regard. Depending upon the state that you plan to hunt, there may be regulations that limit the amount of time required between an over flight of an area and when you can actually begin hunting.

Because of the inherent difficulty of flying in mountainous terrain, it is critical that you never try to do this alone. Mountain flying in the Rockies is nothing like flying over flat farm land and many a wayward pilot has failed to come home because he headed his craft into the mountains with little or no mountain flying training. It's much safer to hire the plane and a competent mountain qualified pilot while you go along as the observer.

*"If you come expecting a fair fight, you are unprepared." ~Unknown*

141

## New Weaponry for Elk Hunters

### Elk Hunting with the Modern Crossbow
One of the hottest new trends in big game hunting today is crossbow
hunting. Crossbows offer big game hunters another option to extend

142

Jay Houston

their season without the requirement of spending months or years to become consistently effective as can be the case with conventional archery tackle.  Additionally crossbows offer lifelong archery hunters who are no longer physically able to draw conventional archery gear, but are not yet ready to become a rifle hunter, a way to remain active in a sport that they have invested years in.

**Barnett Quad Edge S**

While many states offer specific crossbow seasons for big game, currently most limit the use of crossbows to firearm seasons unless the hunter has a physiological reason and documentation from a physician explaining why he or she is unable to use a conventional bow. Over time I expect more states to start offering crossbow specific seasons. In my recently adopted home state of Kentucky, my shoulder surgery limitations and a letter from my doctor allow me to hunt with my crossbow during the entire Kentucky archery deer season which runs from September to January.

Jay Houston

Admittedly, I am new to crossbow hunting. I had been a conventional bowhunter for forty years...until I had to have two shoulder surgeries. Six months of rehab and PT (twice) returned the strength to my shoulders, but the consistency in my shooting was never the same. I continued to bow hunt for a few more years. But after a few misses on bulls that I should have been able to make, I finally accepted the reality that my shoulders were never going to be the same. So I returned to rifle hunting for elk and muleys. Honestly, I love big game hunting any way I can get it, but over the next few years I came to realize how much I missed the up close and personal world of conventional bowhunting.

One Saturday afternoon I was watching a hunting show on The Sportsman's Channel and there was this guy chasing bull elk with a crossbow. Really...that could be me I thought! In about one minute I purposed to learn everything I could about crossbows and crossbow hunting for big game. For nearly six months I scoured the internet, talked to tech reps of major crossbow manufacturers, and picked the brains of everyone I knew that owned a crossbow. A few die hard conventional bowhunters poo-pooed the idea of a crossbow, but most of my elk hunting buds were all for it and excited for my opportunity to return to hunting with anything that shot an arrow.

My trusty PSE compound was still in great shape and I had a friend who was a die-hard outdoorsman that wanted to get into bowhunting. I called up my bud Zac and offered him a deal on all of my bowhunting gear. I knew that Zac had been shopping for a bow for some time and after talking it over with some of his bowhunting friends in Indiana he decided to take me up on my offer. I loaded everything up in the "Elkpedition" and drove to a location about halfway between our respective homes and the deal was done. Cash in hand, my research complete, I called up the folks at Barnett crossbows to locate the

Jay Houston

nearest dealer for my crossbow of choice, the brand new (2015) Quad Edge S crossbow. The Quad Edge S is what I call a mid-priced crossbow. My bow with 6 arrows, bow quiver, 3X32 scope and a soft case set me back right at $500. My out of pocket after the PSE sale, was zero. Two hunters have the rigs they want and I didn't have to break the bank for a new crossbow.  Love horse-trading.

 As is the case with many new products, the marketing guys who put out all the slick ads in magazines and on the Internet that get hunters salivating are usually a step or two or three ahead of the production guys. As it turned out, the Quad Edge S crossbow that I had decided on had not even gone into production yet. Argh......! This sort of thing seems to be the rule rather than the exception for me. Watch for another similar story in the section on the MSR.

After about a dozen calls and emails to as many awesome people at Barnett's production facility in Tarpon Springs, FL my order was finally placed. About a week later UPS shows up at my door with a huge package. The driver, probably a hunter, saw the Barnett return address on the package and had a massive envious grin on his face.

I wasted no time. Getting up to speed with a crossbow was actually fairly straight forward. Once I had a solid understanding of the mechanics and safety considerations, it was only a matter of practice. The basic process of shooting a crossbow is similar to that of firing a rifle. Sight picture, breath control, trigger squeeze was all familiar after years of shooting rifles and shotguns. Range estimation, adjusting for arrow flight path and bow leveling from my days as an archer blended easily with my rifle pre-shot checklist. In just a few hours of practice, I was feeling confident in the use of my new crossbow. One aspect of crossbow shooting that I was not expecting was how blazing fast they appear to be. Crossbow arrows or bolts are much shorter than conventional arrows. Most are in the 18-22 inch range. Mine are 22 inches. My crossbow is advertised to shoot at 350 FPS. That is about 40 FPS faster than my PSE shot. The smaller arrow makes it seem even faster. At 40 yards the arrow impact and trigger release seem to occur simultaneously. I realize that a lot of this is all in my head, but it sure feels like I'm shooting lightning bolts. Speed is good. I like it!

Modern crossbows offer blazing speed with many exceeding 350 FPS and a few topping the 400 FPS threshold. Generally the cost of a crossbow is similar to the cost of conventional compound archery tackle. Starter bows can be found in the $399 range with top of the line crossbows commanding a hefty $1400 or more. The general rule for buying a crossbow is no different than buying a conventional bow, an elk rifle, or a bass boat...buy the best that you can afford. Top brands such as Barnett, Ten-Point, Horton, and Excalibur offer a wide range of crossbows and accessories. Even major players in the compound bow arena such as Hoyt, Matthews and PSE offer multiple lines of crossbows as well.

## Compound Crossbows vs. Recurve Crossbows
In the world of crossbow hunters there are two basic groups of shooters those who prefer the simplicity of a recurve crossbow, and the rest of us. While there are pros and cons to each version, in my opinion it all boils down to personal preference. My choice of a compound crossbow was influenced by three factors: price, speed, and effort required to draw the bow. My Barnett Quad Edge S priced out at $499 retail. For the quality bow I was getting, there was nothing in the recurve community even close. At the time, a comparable crossbow from Excalibur, the leader in recurve crossbows was in the $800 range and the speed for that bow was just 315 FPS.

The recurve community will argue that recurves are lighter, more accurate and more reliable than crossbows with compound limbs. They also argue that compound crossbows are more cumbersome and noisier than recurves.

The compound community argues that within its 40 yard red zone, the speed and ease of movement due to shorter limbs of the compound cannot be matched by the recurve. The compound crossbow shooter has only to draw 50% of the actual draw weight whereas the recurve shooter has to draw the entire weight averaging 150 lbs.

Bottom line, out to the 40 yard mark, shooting a crossbow is not that different that shooting a bench rest rifle allowing the shooter to put arrow after arrow in the virtually the same hole when shooting from a rest. Even experienced compound bow hunters will have difficulty achieving this same level of consistent accuracy.

If you are considering a crossbow purchase, do your homework. Establish a workable budget, and then go out and if possible shoot every crossbow in that price range. Just like selecting a longbow or a compound bow, more often than not, it comes down to personal preference. I would encourage you to stick with crossbow manufacturers that have been in the business for awhile. Time has allowed them to work out the kinks in their designs and engineering. You will be less likely to have to return the bow due to some type of failure.

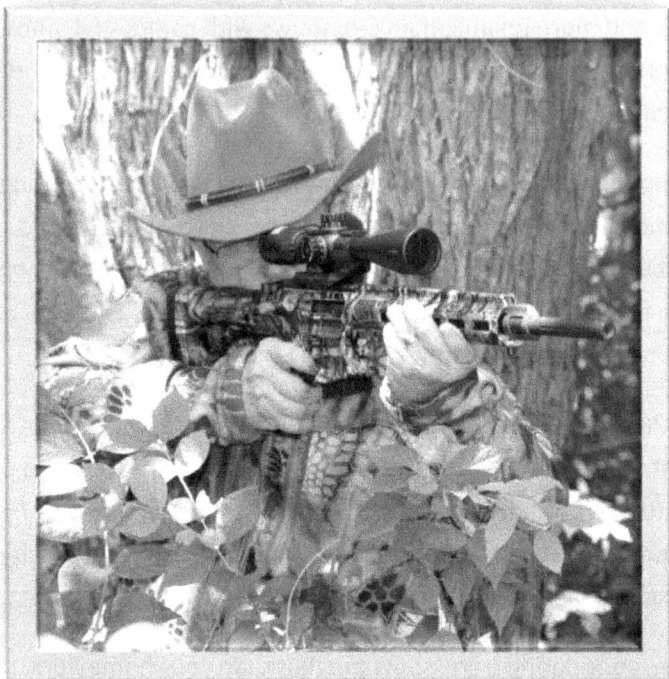

**Elk Hunting with a Modern Sporting Rifle (MSR)**

Longbows, recurve bows, flintlocks, percussion cap muzzleloaders, bolt action, magazine fed, and semi-automatic hunting rifles all evolved from weapons originally designed for the battlefield at one time or another. The most recent addition to this venerable line is the Modern Sporting Rifle or MSR. You may know these better as AR 15 and AR10 type rifles. Today's MSRs are offered in a number of modern calibers suitable for elk including: .308 Winchester, 7MM-08, .300 Blackout, .300 WSM and .338 Federal just to name a few. Additionally there are a host of other big game calibers for the MSR, but they are not in my opinion really suited for taking down elk at longer ranges.

A decade ago when the very first MSRs designed for hunting were just starting to trickle into the market, the conversations about their suitability for big game such as deer, bear and elk became downright heated at times. Like anything else, time becomes the true measure and today MSRs have a well respected and solid reputation as reliable hunting rifles.

A quick look at the firearms market [2017]reveals that major firearm manufacturers have made a commitment to MSRs.

- Remington R-25 G2, Available in: .243 Win, .308 Win, 7mm-08, .300 Blackout
- DPMS Lite Hunter, Available in: .243 Win, .260, 308 Win, 7mm-08, .300 Blackout
- Ruger Arms ST-762, Available in: .308 Win/7.62
- Stag Arms 6.8 SPC Model 17
- Colt LE 901-16S, Available in: .308 Win
- JP Enterprises LRP-07H, Available in: .338 Federal
- LaRue Tactical OBR 7.62

One significant advantage of hunting with an MSR over a more conventional bolt gun is the ability to get off a follow up shot much faster. Elk hunters learn quickly that these critters are tough and simply do not go down immediately even with a well placed double-lung shot. A wise old outfitter convinced me early in my elk hunting career that a DRT elk is far easier to pack out than one you have to chase for a mile or more. His philosophy and mine as well is to keep shooting until the animal is down to stay. If you are shooting a bolt gun that requires breaking the bolt open, extracting the spent round, chambering a new round and reacquiring the target for the follow up shot. With an MSR, the shooter doesn't even need to take his eye from the scope. He just needs to resettle the crosshair and take the follow up shot.

**Remington R-25 G II with Nikon P-308 Optics**

MSRs are gas operated and as such are designed to minimize effective recoil. On a bolt rifle, a large percentage of the recoil is absorbed by the shooter's shoulder. (This can be as much as 4X that of an MSR) On MSRs the rifle absorbs a large amount of the recoil as the gas is used to assist in cycling the action.

While the weight of an MSR is not that different than that of a stainless steel barrel/action bolt gun, MSRs as a rule are more compact than bolt guns making for easier transport. My personal rig, a Remington R-25 GII with Nikon P-308 optics weighs in at 8.7

pounds empty, whereas my Stainless Remington Model 700LSS with optics tips the scales at just over 10 pounds. MSRs are also designed to be carried using a single point harness that keeps the weapon in a ready position in front of the shooter rather than behind the shooter on his shoulder as is the case with most bolt guns.

Finally, many of today's MSRs can be converted to another caliber with little effort and very affordable costs. Today's .308 elk or deer shooter can become tomorrow's .243 varmint rifle.

## The Latest in Traditional Archery Technology
## Bill Carmen

*Many thanks again to my good friend Bill Carmen for this highly informative piece on traditional bowhunting gear.*

"Traditional" and "Technology" are words you typically do not use in the same sentence. Today's traditional archery equipment may have that beautiful wood grain look, but unless it is hand-carved from  hickory or Osage orange, make no mistake about it, it is high-tech. Believe me, it's not your granddaddy's bow!

Traditional archery has made quite the resurgence in the past decade. If you pick up an issue of *Traditional Bowhunter Magazine*, there are no less than seventy advertisements from companies and individuals who are making traditional bows, arrows, and tackle.  Companies like Easton, Wasp, Muzzy, Hoyt, Martin and Bear, outfits who for years catered almost exclusively to the compound bow market, now have a significant presence among traditional bowhunting equipment makers.   Even custom handcrafted traditional bows use modern materials and components. For instance, my favorite bow, a takedown Black Widow recurve, despite having elegant lines and beautiful wood patterns, utilizes the latest in impregnations, laminations and modern adhesives to hold it all together. Many companies like Hoyt are using carbon laminations and a few, like DAS and Tomahawk, are using syntactic foam laminations. Most good bow strings are now high-tech special polyester that has very little stretch, which increases bow efficiency.

My "go-to" arrows, at first glance, appear to be slim wooden shafts with the grain clearly visible. They are not. They are Easton Traditional Only carbon fiber arrows with a wood grain pattern printed on each shaft using a process called PhotoFusion. These arrows have a smaller diameter than wood arrows of the same weight and spine, which increases penetration. And, of course, the weight, spine, and straightness are much more consistent from arrow to arrow. There are several companies now making similar products. The result is archery equipment that is beautiful, functional, and can be shot the same way Fred Bear or Howard Hill shot, but packs a bigger punch.

Use a modern traditional bow, and choose arrows and broadheads based on penetration research by Dr. Ed Ashby and others in that field. Then you'll have a lethal weapon that will match or outperform any bow of any type on the market today and is capable of harvesting any big game animal on earth.

I often kid around with my good buddy, Eric Crook, who is one of the best hunters I know. He shoots a compound bow and I chide him for using a bow with training wheels. He immediately fires back at me with an interesting comparison. Otzi, the Neolithic hunter whose mummified body was discovered in a snow bank in the Alps in 1991, was carrying archery equipment and a primitive axe. Otzi's equipment literally rewrote the history books on our knowledge of early technology. Previous archaeology led us to believe that 5,000 years ago, humans did not yet have the capability to make metal equipment. And yet this early iceman had a copper axe. It was roughly the same size and shape of contemporary stone axes, but it was made of copper, a high-tech accomplishment at the time. And, Otzi's arrows are the first evidence we have that early archers used spiral fletching.  Eric's argument is that even five thousand years ago, human hunters, using "traditional" designs, were experimenting with new technology.

Why use traditional archery equipment when space-age compound bows are available at comparable prices? If you have any eye for beauty, it's easy to see the artistic grace in the lines of a traditional bow. It is much faster for a traditional archer to aim and shoot, because the "aiming" occurs without bowsights during the process of drawing the bow. When the arrow touches the archer's cheek the arrow is released. Traditional bows are low-maintenance. There are no sights, screws, cams, pulleys, tools, or Allen wrenches.  You just go hunting.  And lastly, hunting with traditional equipment is a celebration of our heritage…from Agincourt to Fred Bear.

With all of that said, I still do occasionally hunt with a wood self-bow that has no laminations. I also use real wood arrows. But without apology, I most often enjoy the equipment that invokes the best of both worlds….the traditional archery ambience and methods of our forefathers with the technology that makes those methods more lethal.

So, if after you killed your last deer or elk with a compound bow, you muttered something like, "Oh well…I just shot another one," you might be ready for the challenge of traditional archery. But you can rest assured that the technology of today's traditional bows and arrows is quite capable of the task.

## Hunting Western Elk Populations, Top OTC States

The top three western states offering over the counter (OTC) elk tags include Colorado, Idaho and Oregon. **Colorado** is home to the largest elk population by far in the western US hosting a herd of nearly 300,000 elk. If you are looking for quantity over quality, Colorado is definitely your best option. Elk in Colorado are hunted hard due to its popularity. It is a prime elk hunting destination which has resulted in a prevalence of younger bulls.  A young 240-270 B&C bull makes for some appetizing

Jay Houston

eating for the meat hunter. If you are looking to harvest a nice fat cow for the freezer, again you are in luck. In most units cow elk make up 80-85 percent of the herd. You will need to put in for the draw and be successful however, as cow tags are all draw tags. The exception being private land vouchers and leftover tags which are available after all draw awards are complete. Colorado also has more OTC units called GMU or Game Management Units than any other Western state. Colorado has 147 units available to hunt with a bow and 92 units to hunt with a rifle. The cost of an elk tag in Colorado will run a non-resident right at $636.00 [2016].

If you are looking to hunt true [B&C] trophy bulls in Colorado, look primarily to private ranches in the south central part of the state around Trinidad, or GMUs 1, 2, 10 or 201 in the northwest part of the state. If GMU 201 is your target, start putting in for preference points early and be prepared to wait. Currently it takes about 19 preference points for a resident to draw. Hunting in these units positions the hunter to harvest bulls in the 360 plus range, with 380 or better class bulls a real possibility. There are also some very select opportunities for harvesting 350-360 class bulls on private land in south central Colorado and southern New Mexico. Hunt prices [2017] here can range from $8500-$10,500 per hunter and may require the hunter to place his name on a wait list for as long as two years as the demand for these exceptional opportunities far exceeds the supply of hunts each year. Yep, that is a lot of money, but it is the cost of the ticket, if one wants to play in the trophy bull game without waiting a lifetime to draw using preference points as many of these opportunities include a landowner voucher that allows the hunter to purchase a tag without points.

Jay Houston

Finally, I would be remiss if I failed to mention the White River National Forest. This is the #1 elk hunting area in the state, possibly in the entire country, and attracts more elk hunters than any other. The resident elk herd is estimated to be around 30,000 animals. For hunters who are willing to do what it takes to get into the elk and are comfortable hunting with a lot of other hunters, GMUs 12 and 24 are excellent positions to begin your search for that killer elk spot.

Next on the list is **Idaho**. Seventy percent of Idaho is public land, and elk are found in every type of terrain. A back country elk hunt in Idaho's national forests is a dream for any hunter. With an elk population of approximately 120,000 elk, Idaho is an outstanding elk hunting state offering opportunities on mature bulls with low to moderate hunting pressure. My only warning is that some of the best hunting is found in the northern part of the state where terrain can be brutal. Elk hunting is managed in 28 elk zones with a 2-tag system in most zones - A tag & B tag. In general, 'A tags' provide more opportunity for muzzleloader and archery hunters and B tags provide more opportunity for center fire rifle hunters. Hunters may select one zone and choose either an A tag or a B tag. Idaho offers 87 units available to hunt over the counter. You will have your choice of rifle, muzzleloader, or archery. The total cost for a tag to hunt in Idaho as a non-resident is about $570.00. I hunted unit 7 in the Idaho panhandle a few years ago and all the bulls we encountered were 6x6 or better. In the entire time I was there, other than our party, I saw only one other hunting camp. Idaho Fish and Game offers hunt planning tools that can be found online at: https://fishandgame.idaho.gov/ifwis/huntPlanner.

Finally, the last western OTC state on our list is **Oregon**. Oregon has an elk herd of 125,000. There are Rocky Mountain elk found in eastern

Oregon and Roosevelt elk are found in the western parts of the state. Rifle hunting is general season in western Oregon for the most part, except for some coastal units where it's controlled hunting. There is one week-long general season hunt with a spike only bag limit in parts of NE Oregon (Rocky Mt Elk 2nd season), but remaining eastern Oregon seasons are controlled. All the general rifle elk seasons take place in October and November. Archery elk hunting is general season nearly statewide and coincides with general archery deer season. The bag limit is one elk in many units. Season opens on a Saturday in late August and runs 30 days, ending on a Sunday in late September. Some controlled archery hunts are also available. Muzzleloader controlled hunts are available. New in 2016, a Premium Elk Hunt is available in almost all wildlife management units. Hunters who <u>draw</u> this special tag can hunt Sept. 1-Nov. 30. *Field and Stream* Magazine named the Siuslaw National Forest as the best public elk hunting land in the country. It comprises 600,000 acres of woodlands absolutely crawling with Rocky Mountain elk. Siuslaw is located on the coast and Oregon is a notoriously wet state. When the rain is falling, elk tend to stay under cover. However, if you are willing to wait out the storms and put in some quality time getting to know the area, Siuslaw will reward you with an awesome opportunity for harvesting your bull. Another area located on the eastern side of the state is the Umatilla National Forest drawing some 30,000 hunters a year. In 2015, ODFW offered about 60,000 controlled elk tags. A 2016 non-resident tag will set you back just over $700.00. If you are looking to position yourself to harvest a Roosevelt bull, the dense forests of western Oregon are your best bet.

Jay Houston

**Steven Rinella, MeatEater, Kentucky**

## Hunting Eastern Elk Populations

Thanks to the foresight, diligence and just plain hard work of many state wildlife agencies, universities, landowners, non-profits like the Rocky Mountain Elk Foundation and conservation minded individuals, wild free-ranging elk populations are in the process of being restored to many of their former ranges east of the Mississippi river. Today elk are making tracks in places where they haven't for more than a century.

158

Jay Houston

**PENNSYLVANIA** has 13 established elk zones for which antlered and antlerless elk tags may be allocated each year. Licenses are allocated by lottery (draw). As conservationists discovered when an effort was made to stock elk in the rich agricultural lands of western Kentucky, farmers and elk don't always get along too well, and farmers can vote. Agricultural interests in Pennsylvania fought against restoration efforts for several decades, until various compromises more or less ensured that elk would stay away from most farmlands. Pennsylvania's restocking program has forged ahead and now hunting is allowed on public lands in the north-central part of the state.

Pennsylvania's first elk hunt in modern times took place in 2001 when 30 permits were issued. In 2015, 21 antlered and 95 antlerless permits were issued after a drawing that takes place in August. The application process costs $10.70 to enter. The season typically occurs in early to mid November. If drawn, your non-resident elk tag will set you back a mere $250.00. Compared to the cost of a western elk tag, this is a steal.

**ARKANSAS** The permit application period for public lands elk hunts occurs May 1-June 1 and ends for private lands on July 15. The only elk zone for private land is in Boone, Carroll, Madison, Newton, and Searcy counties. Application fees are $35 to apply for one of the 12 bull and 24 antlerless permits available. The Arkansas herd is estimated at less than 1,000 animals, mostly scattered across private lands in the wild Ozark region of the north. For more information visit the Arkansas Game and Fish Commission website.

**TENNESSEE** The state charges $10 to enter the annual drawing for a permit, plus $2 if it's done by internet. However, only four elk-hunting permits are available. A fifth permit is provided to a conservation organization such as the Rocky Mountain Elk Foundation as a fundraising tool. A quota permit system is used to select most of the elk hunt participants. The elk hunt takes place on North Cumberland WMA, located in the Cumberland Mountains of eastern Tennessee. Seven Elk Hunting Zones (EHZs) have been designated on the North Cumberland WMA. The Five EHZs open for the 2015 Elk Season were EHZ 2, 3, 5, 6 and 7. Each of the five hunters is assigned a separate EHZ. The youth hunter is allowed to use all five open EHZs. If you want a permit, apply in mid July; the season takes place in mid October at North Cumberland WMA in Scott County. Seven elk hunting zones have been designated on the North Cumberland Wildlife Management Area (WMA), as follows:

EHZ 1: Chestnut Ridge and Fork Mountain: That portion of the North Cumberland WMA west of I-75 and east of the Southern railroad tracks. All safety zones designated by TWRA and private property excluded.

EHZ 2: Adkins and Turkey Mountain: That portion west of the Southern railroad tracks, east of Red Ash Rd. to Wheeler Gap, northeast of Adkins Mountain Rd. to Jenny Gap, east of Straight Fork Rd. to State Highway 63, east of Highway 63 to the Southern railroad tracks. All safety zones designated by TWRA and private property excluded.

EHZ 3: Horse Gap and Wolf Ridge: That portion of North Cumberland WMA south of Adkins Mountain Rd. to Huckaby Knob, west of the trail on Brushy Mountain Ridge to Montgomery Fork Creek, north of Fork Creek (downstream) to the North Cumberland WMA boundary line and east of the North Cumberland WMA boundary line to Jenny Gap. All safety zones designated by TWRA and private property excluded.

EHZ 4: Anderson and Massengale Mountain: That portion on the North Cumberland WMA south of Montgomery Fork Creek to Little Bruce Ridge, west of Little Bruce Ridge to Short Haul Rd. to Grave Gap, north

160

of Massengale Mountain road to Poor Mountain Rd., north of Poor Mountain Rd. to Norma Rd. to Montgomery Fork Creek. All safety zones designated by TWRA and private property excluded.

EHZ 5: Cross Mountain and Red Ash: That portion on the North Cumberland WMA south of Red Ash Rd. to Wheeler Gap, west of Adkins Mountain Rd. to Huckaby Knob, east of the trail on the Brushy Mountain Ridge to Montgomery Fork Creek, east of Little Bruce Ridge to Short Haul Rd., east of Massengale Rd. to Ash Log Gap, north of boundary back to Southern railroad, west of Southern railroad to Red Ash Church. All safety zones designated by TWRA and private property excluded.

EHZ 6: Braden Mountain: That portion of the North Cumberland WMA north of State Highway 63, west of State Highway 297, and east of the Rock House community. EHZ 6 also includes the Mon Petit/Atlas Petroleum property which joins the North Cumberland boundary on the north. All safety zones designated by TWRA and private property excluded.

EHZ 7: Tackett Creek: That portion of the North Cumberland WMA south of Tennessee and the Kentucky State Line, north of the Cumberland Mountain State Park Trail and east of State Highway 25W. All safety zones designated by TWRA and private property excluded.

Source: Tennessee Wildlife Resources Agency

**VIRGINIA**

As of this writing, Virginia's elk hunting program appears to be an extension of the state's deer hunting program. Anyone who has a valid hunting license and permits can shoot an elk of either sex if they have the opportunity during deer season. The exception is the zone in

Buchanan, Dickenson, and Wise counties, which is where most of the elk stocked in the state's southwestern coalfield as part of a restoration program currently reside. Still, a few wandering elk are taken outside the area each year. Virginia's original plan called for a managed elk-hunting season to begin within five years of the last stocking. However, elk are still being stocked, so it might be a while yet. For additional information visit the Virginia Department of Game and Fisheries.

**KENTUCKY**

Kentucky's permit application period runs from Jan. 1 through April 30 each year, and is well worth the $10 per application to enter. For 2017, elk hunters can apply in each of four drawing pools for these coveted tags: Archery antlered and antlerless, and Rifle antlered and antlerless. The 2015 Telecheck results indicate that Knott County had the largest harvest by a wide margin with 138 animals harvested followed by Leslie, Perry and Martin counties. By far, the Bluegrass State has been the most successful with elk restoration and now has a herd estimated at more than 11,000, which makes it the 10th largest herd in the country according to the Rocky Mountain Elk Foundation. Plenty of bulls scoring in the high 300s have been taken in the state, including the state gun record of 372 6/8 harvested in 2009 and the state archery record of 361 5/8 tagged in 2014. The elk zone now consists of 16 counties, a far cry from the days when the first animals were brought into the Commonwealth and kept at Land Between the Lakes in the western part of the state. Though they were never released at LBL, beginning in 2002 that small herd became the seed stock for elk released in the reclaimed strip mine land of the eastern mountains. Now a number of other states are relying on Kentucky to provide elk. In Kentucky it's legal to shoot an elk during deer season if it wanders outside the established elk zone. A hunter must possess a valid hunting license and an out-of-zone elk permit: $30 for residents, $400 for nonresidents. For additional information visit the Kentucky Department of Fish and Wildlife Resources.

## FUTURE EASTERN ELK HUNTING STATES

### WEST VIRGINIA
The state has been trying to kick-start an elk-reintroduction program for several decades. In 2014 the Rocky Mountain Elk Foundation pledged a $50,000 grant to the state for that purpose. In a public meeting, expressions of support for reintroduction were overwhelming. As is the case in Virginia and Kentucky, elk will be released onto reclaimed mine land in the mountainous area of the south where run-ins with farmers and vehicles are apt to be minimal. In West Virginia, that's McDowell (across the state line from Virginia's Buchanan County), Wyoming, Logan, and Mingo counties plus southern Boone, Lincoln, and Wayne counties. For more information visit the Division of Natural Resources' site.

### MISSOURI
In 2010, Missouri's Department of Conservation began an elk restoration in the southern part of that state on the Peck Ranch Conservation Area in Shannon, Carter, and Reynolds counties. In May 2011, the first elk were transported from eastern Kentucky to Missouri to begin the project. It's still going to be a while before the Missouri herd has reached a size that will allow hunting to be applied as a management tool.

### OTHER STATES
In June of 2015, the first 28 of 150 elk that Wisconsin will acquire from Kentucky were transported north as the former's restocking program

got underway. It's in the works, as it is in New York and a couple of other states.

Outside of the Bluegrass state, elk hunting isn't well established in the eastern US. However, people do draw permits and harvest elk there. If you hadn't thought about hunting elk in the eastern U.S, maybe you should.

## "Stuff" is the New Term for Gear

As you are backing the truck out of the driveway your spouse gets your text, "I'm going to run into town and grab some stuff for my elk hunt. I

165

won't be gone long." Sound familiar? How many times does this or something closely resembling it get repeated across America in the months leading up to elk season? I'm sure this is both a guy thing and a hunter thing. Since I'm both, it is impossible for me to separate the two. Suffice it to say that most elk hunters that I've encountered are addicts to the activity. Along with the obsessions associated with being an elk hunter come an associated appetite to acquire new and better "stuff." Stuff by the way is the new term for gear.

So how much "stuff" is enough? For most hunters of all types there is no such thing as enough. There is always one more piece of stuff that the elk hunter "needs." If you were to open the garage door at my house, you would see a lot of stuff. Front to back, left to right, and in no particular order, almost every nook and cranny is filled, piled, or stacked with stuff that I use (or used) for elk hunting. Tents, camp stoves, boots, clothing, tarps, ropes, generators, the list goes on. Admittedly a lot of this stuff never moves, not even to elk camp, but you can be sure that at some point in the past, it was "necessary stuff." Some folks are caught up in the accumulation of wealth; elk hunters are usually caught up in the accumulation of "stuff."

Like so many writers who have come before me, as well as those that will follow, I realize that any discussion on hunting gear preferences is a recipe for trouble. No matter how hard one tries to be generic, open-minded, non-preferential, or whatever, someone out there is going to take issue with your point of view or opinion. So that having been said, keep in mind that the following is just that: one elk hunter's opinion or point of view.

Jay Houston

## Apparel

Collectively with a good pair of broken-in waterproof boots, a durable functional clothing plan for your hunt is critical for any successful elk hunt. Weather in elk country is finicky and it **WILL** change on you in a heartbeat. Just when you think you're prepared for a warm day during your September bow hunt and head out of camp with nothing on but light-weight gear, an unpredicted upslope or Albuquerque low will blow in and wham, you're miles from the truck, snow is flying sideways, and the temperature may be dropping ten degrees an hour. This is not good! Repeat NOT GOOD! If your clothing plan doesn't take into account the possibility of unanticipated inclement weather, you could be in for some serious trouble...or worse. I'm not a doctor, but it doesn't take one to know that if your internal core body temperature starts to drop, it doesn't have to go far before hypothermia will begin to set in which can be life threatening.

## Kryptek – The Secret Weapon in High-tech Apparel for Elk Hunters

In recent years, the hunting apparel industry has exploded producing a broad array of new high-tech fabrics and systems that provide outstanding insulation without the associated weight or discomfort of older bulky clothing. A select few of these new designs and systems have been adapted for hunting from lessons learned during military field ops in Iraq and Afghanistan as well as from other outdoor sports such as mountaineering and backpacking. Two huge advantages of these new systems are durable yet lightweight fabrics and reduced volume. Trust me; I have tried most all of them over the years. These days my favorite hunting gear hands down is produced by the folks at **Kryptek Outdoor Group** in Eagle, Idaho. Before I share why I believe so much in Kryptek's systems, let's briefly discuss why is it critical to have no-fail top-notch clothing systems when you are hunting.

167

Hypothermia is defined as core body temperature lower than 95 degrees. That is a mere 3.6 degrees lower than what is considered normal for most humans. When one's core temperature drops farther down to 90, you are considered to be in mild hypothermia. Symptoms include uncontrollable shivering. A person in this state of hypothermia will be pale and cool. They will exhibit varying degrees of confusion and incoherence, and experience trouble in making movements. Below 90 degrees, blood pressure, heart rate, and respiration decrease and the shivering reflex is gone. That's when hypothermia becomes really dangerous. Shivering creates heat, and once the shivering ceases there's nothing creating heat. You're just lying there. Your body is basically going to cool to ambient temperature and death is inevitable unless you get help. Hypothermia can be a very real threat for any hunter. You don't have to be ten miles into the backcountry above timberline to encounter this silent killer.

A time-tested strategy to effectively deal with unpredictable weather and avoid the effects of hypothermia that can be encountered while elk hunting is to use a system approach, in essence dressing using layers. This allows the hunter to strip off or add on clothing throughout the day as temperatures or other weather factors may dictate. I typically hunt from late October to mid November when daytime temperatures in the high country can range from a frigid low of 10 degrees to a more tropical even sweltering 70 degrees. I have to be prepared for it all every time I head out.

My system plan is usually something like this: Over my undergarments, I wear a light-weight form fitting layer of moisture-wicking antimicrobial merino wool/spandex.  This keeps me dry and as scent free as possible. I don't use any commercial scent blocker system as most use activated carbon to absorb odors. Once the activated carbon layer is saturated (about one day in elk country), the only way to make it effective again is to heat it in a dryer...and I rarely have access to a dryer on my elk hunts. Thus you end up hunting in a lot of stinky gear thinking you are bullet-proof from a scent management point of view.

My choice is a Kryptek Hoplite Merino wool baselayer. Most hunters agree about the value of wool blends in cold weather, but let me share the results of a recent filed-test I did in HOT weather. It was July and the outside temp ranged from 82 to 86 degrees that particular morning. I decided to put on my Hoplite long sleeve baselayer 1/4 zip top just to see what would happen. In the three hours I had it on out in the heat; I was never hot or even uncomfortable. Conveniently, a quick rinse in a creek will remove most if not all the odor. Just hang it up to dry overnight.

Ok back to the system. Over my baselayer I wear my outer pants (see below) and a medium weight top garment or shirt followed by a wind/water proof jacket, always in camo. I cannot tell you how many times I've sat on a hill side or ridgeline glassing opposite slopes for elk on a frosty October morning, and thanked God that He gave me the good sense to spend the extra money on gear that keeps me dry and blocks out the wind. I don't know why, but it seems as if that first hour after sunrise can be far more windy and cold than sitting in the dark waiting for the sun to come up. The wind resistant pants and shirt are followed by an insulated jacket or parka with some type of water repellant outer layer. Some folks prefer a waist length jacket. On warmer or even moderate temperature days, I'm all with a shorter lighter-weight top layer too. On the other hand, if I expect to encounter harsh snowy or icy weather with even a little wind, I have found that the extra length of a parka helps to prevent cold air from blowing up my back during those early morning hours when the wind is moving down the mountain against my back. If you've ever had a gust of cold alpine air blow up the back of your hunting jacket, you know what I mean. If the weather is pretty cold in the morning, I may also put on another light-weight blended layer over my shirt, planning to take it off and store it in my daypack as the day warms up.

A quick story here may help to reinforce the value of wearing first-class gear. It was opening day of Colorado's first elk season. My hunting partner, his son, and I had hiked for about an hour and a half to our pre-scouted spot. It had snowed somewhere between four and six inches during the night, which had frozen over and made for a somewhat noisy walk as our boots cracked like breaking glass through the crust of snow with every step. Our spirits were high, because we knew the snow would help to move the elk. As we approached the patch of low-lying Juniper that we had planned to use as cover, a freezing North wind began to blow. Within just a couple of minutes the weather had gone from dead calm but cold, to freezing with 40 miles per hour wind and snow blowing sideways across us. Sitting on a bare mountainside above timberline with only those tiny ground-hugging Junipers to shield us from the wind, we must have been a pretty comical sight, as we tried to get out of the driving wind and snow. My hunting partner and his son were huddled up about a hundred yards north of me. I had unzipped the collar of my parka and pulled out the stuffed hood and drawn it down tight over my watch cap leaving just enough open space over my nose to breathe. Then, I found a Juniper about sixteen inches high and did my best to get behind or underneath it... anywhere to get out of that hurricane-like wind and snow. I cannot recall ever being so thankful for having thought ahead and planned for such a remote possibility as I experienced on that bitterly cold and bracing opening day.

I have spent most of my adult life living and hunting in the West. Most old timer elk guides, packers, and cooks...the folks who spend months, not just days at a time in every climate imaginable swear by wool. Why? Because they are highly resistant to change and wool has been the standard for high-country outdoor apparel for over a century. Wool can keep you cool when its warm and it will keep you warm when the temps take a nose dive. If you get cold, put on more wool these folks will say. Wool is much more resistant to moisture than is cotton but once wool becomes saturated...it stays saturated. Realistically the only way to dry it out is to hang it up near a fire or in a warm tent overnight. Another major disadvantage of older heavy wool products however is weight. Due to its density, older wool products can be much heavier than some of their newer high-tech counterparts. From a personal note, I can't stand to have pure wool against my skin. The itching drives me nuts. If you buy high quality wool clothing this will not be an issue because the manufacturer knows this and designs the garment with blends and liners around sensitive areas like the neck, sleeves, and sometime liners for pant legs to prevent this very problem. So the lesson here is, if you are going to go for wool, go for a merino wool blend and don't go cheap.

Durability and flexibility are additional requirements that can make the difference between a successful hunt and a busted hunt. Your average cheap big box camo hunting apparel is made from cotton or in some rare cases a poly-cotton blend. Cotton has in my opinion virtually no insulation value regardless of how many layers you add on. When cotton gets wet, it stays wet. Cotton is highly absorbent meaning that when your outer cotton layer gets wet; it will continue to wick through each successive layer until that moisture finally makes its way to your skin. This will add to the effects of hypothermia. Cotton is not flexible, meaning that garments made of cotton will not flex as you put stress on it moving through elk country. Finally, cotton is the least durable of all fabrics used in the manufacture of hunting clothing. So why do we continue to see it line the shelves every hunting season....because it is cheap, folks! Years ago, before I learned about the many failings of cotton as an effective material for hunting apparel, I was lucky to have a set of gear last more than one or two seasons. Over time every stress point you can think of blew out leaving me in search of a cheap fix, which was usually...more cheap cotton gear.  In 2008 I was introduced to new ultra light-weight synthetic durable water resistant hunting clothing at a hunting show.  Apparently mountain climbers had been using this stuff successfully for years. Now it was available in camo. Needless to say, after a bit of research, I ditched all my old cotton stuff and switched to one of these new systems.

I have been hunting in the same "stuff" for the past eight years [now 2016]. In that time two things have changed that dictated that I needed to consider getting some new gear. First was my waistline (we all understand this...enough said). Second was that there are now incredible newer state-of-the-art clothing systems on the market. These offer even more protection, greater durability and customization for the individual hunter that my old "new" stuff just couldn't deliver; and at the time this was top of the line gear.

My research began like so many previous efforts with my clothing checklist of "gotta haves." For me these are requirements and are nonnegotiable.

- **Extremely durable high-quality construction**
- **Ultra quiet flexible (stretch) materials**
- **Comfortable in a wide range of environments and conditions**
- **Lots of pockets, pit zips and access points**
- **A total system approach offering everything from next to my skin to outer layers**
- **A camo strategy that would be effective in almost any environment**

As I was not in a hurry I took my time doing the research. My last system lasted eight years. My goal for the new system is at least another eight years. That is a fairly lofty challenge for a garment that is sure to get its share of abuse. By nature I am a skeptic. For me new stuff is always questionable until I have tested it thoroughly. After almost six months of research and testing, I was convinced that my **Kryptek Highlander** system not only met my requirements, it exceeded them.

I am a vet. If you leave the military with anything of value it is the knowledge that your fellow vets will always have your back. FOREVER! I am also a huge believer in doing business with veteran owned businesses whenever possible. Kryptek is veteran owned and managed by men who stood shoulder to shoulder in the Battlespace in Iraq and Afghanistan. In all honesty, this was one of the deciding factors that led to my choice of gear.

Due to the times of year and environments I typically hunt in, I chose two distinct systems, one for moderately cold weather and one for harsh cold weather. My **Kryptek Cadog** system has proven to be outstanding for mid to late October still hunting above 6000' where I experienced temps in the 30-60 degree range.  If I expect to put on some serious miles I go light and fast, preferring to just carry my weapon and a backpack hydration system forgoing the extra weight and bulk of a daypack. My Kryptek Cadog kit provides me this flexibility as it is lightweight, provides excellent insulation and there are pockets and zips EVERYWHERE for food and small gear. Additionally, every joint and contact point is reinforced for durability. I chose **Kryptek's Highlander** camo pattern because its multi-layered patterns and colors work as well above timberline as below in darker timber. Plus in my opinion, it is hands down just the coolest Sierra Hotel looking pattern on the market.

Let me share a quick word about effective camo patterns. For decades hunting camo was designed to mimic nature, specifically imitating patterns and colors of leaves and branches...mostly found in eastern forests. The guys at Kryptek took a new ground-breaking approach to camouflage design. They utilize innovative high-tech multi-level layering techniques in their patterns by incorporating shading and random geometrical foregrounds to create a three-dimensional effect that ensures maximum concealment at both close and long ranges.

Recently a hunting buddy of mine field tested one of those well known nature patterns. He hiked up a ridgeline about a quarter of a mile from the observer and crouched in front of some Juniper scrub. Via his phone he asked the observer to try to find him. In about five seconds the observer told him exactly where he was standing and that he was clearly visible. The pattern had failed to do its job of concealment.  I figured if it worked once, perhaps I should try a similar test., but I decided to step it up a little and test my Kryptek Highlander not once or twice but in five distinct settings: hard timber, open range, rocky

174

terrain, in a tree stand, and sitting at the base of a lone tree on a ridgeline. In every case, the observer was unable to locate me. Every time I had to talk his eyes onto my location and even with this help, on three occasions…he never saw me until I stood and waived my arms to get his attention. Winner Kryptek!

Here are a few specs for this great gear:

**Cadog Jacket Features:**

- Mechanical stretch woven fabric
- DWR water resistant
- Internal sleeve cuffs
- Chest pockets
- Arm pockets
- Pit zips
- Fleece backing
- Stretch fabric
- Jacket hem pull cords
- Camo

**Cadog Pant Features:**

- DWR water resistant
- Bonded laminate reinforced knees
- Fleece backing
- Stretch fabric
- Low profile waist adjustment system
- Suspender compatible
- Knee pad pockets
- Articulated athletic fit
- Mechanical stretch woven soft shell bonded
- Camo

When I anticipate spending long periods of time in harsh or even freezing conditions or when I expect to sit on a freezing cold deer stand for long hours at a time, I don my **Kryptek Aegis Extreme Cold Weather** system. It is 100% windproof/waterproof and insulated with Primaloft®. Guys, I inherited poor circulation from my mom, so if I get really cold …I'm done. Hunting is a huge part of my life and I am not going to risk my hunt to temperature or inclement weather. My stuff is critical. If that means that I have to spend more to get the best, I am more than willing to do so. For me, the cost of a busted hunt due to my inability to endure the environment is totally unacceptable. I am just not going to risk it.  You probably know what I mean. You have been patterning that bull or buck all summer. You have hundreds of hours and miles invested in bringing him to ground. With so much of your life invested, gear is not the place to shortchange yourself by possibly blowing up your entire hunt. Just make the investment. You will not regret it.

**Aegis Extreme Jacket Features:**

- 10,000mm waterproof properties
- Primaloft insulation
- Stretch fabric
- Durable fabric
- 100% waterproof & windproof
- Body mapping insulation
- Waterproof zippers
- Pit zips
- Jacket hem pull cords
- Internal chest pockets
- Removable hood
- Camo

**Aegis Extreme Bib Features:**

- Primaloft®
- Stretch fabric
- 100% waterproof & windproof
- Body mapping insulation
- Articulated athletic fit
- Full leg zip
- Bonded laminate reinforced knees
- Camo

**Boots Will Make or Break Your Elk Hunt**

This may be the most to the point discussion on gear that you find anywhere in this book. In my opinion, a well designed, quality built, waterproof, pair of boots that fit correctly is one of, if not the most essential item on the elk hunter's gear checklist. Nothing… I mean nothing will end an elk hunt faster than having your feet fail you because of poor planning in the footwear department. Becoming a successful elk hunter requires that you have the ability to go long and stay out long. This means having the capacity and gear to literally walk as much as ten miles in unforgiving terrain every day. To do this day in and day out requires that you prioritize taking good care of your feet and ankles.

I have heard the guys who say that they hunt in tennis shoes because they are comfortable and quiet. Folks, I just don't buy it. Why would anyone risk ruining an elk hunt for which they have waited all year or maybe a lifetime by blowing out an ankle or blistering up their feet just to be more comfortable or a bit sneakier in a pair of tennis shoes? A good pair of well designed boots combined with some careful walking and planning will accomplish the same degree of comfort and quiet,

177

while giving your feet and ankles the support and protection that they will need while hunting the ups and downs of elk country.

**Elk Hunter Tip: Everything you take into the field; your rifle or bow, your backpack, your camo gear, your food, yourself, everything is piled on top of your boots. The bottom line is: don't go cheap on your boots.**

### Choosing the Right Elk Rifle for You

At ElkCamp.com I have received hundreds of inquiries from hunters wanting my opinion on what is the best elk rifle. For all of you who have been holding your breath, here is my answer. In my opinion, the absolute best rifle that you can have for elk hunting is the largest caliber rifle that you can shoot consistently. I had to include the largest caliber criteria in there because sure is shootin', some guy will ask if a 5.56 mm or .223  AR will suffice. No, a .223 will not suffice for elk. In Colorado where I hunt primarily, the regulations stipulate that a legal elk rifle "must be .24 caliber (6mm) or more." In my opinion even that is far too light a load for elk.

OK, now that we have excluded all the gopher whackers that leaves quite a range of boomers to choose from. A few years back, we took a poll of our readers at elkcamp.com on which rifle caliber folks preferred for elk hunting. In the six months that we made the poll available, nearly 750 people responded with their opinions. Of those surveyed more than 80 percent argued that bigger was better, with either the 7MM Remington Magnum or some version of the .300 Magnums being the preferred calibers of choice.

As I get older, I find that I am less and less inclined to have to chase or track an elk for miles after the shot. My preference would be to have the brute's knees drop out from under him and plant him right there (DRT). In the back of my truck is even better. Conventional thinking leads you to believe that if an elk is hit by a larger caliber round moving at 2500 FPS or better, that he will stay put. Unfortunately, this is not always the case. Real life confirms that many elk even when hit by long time elk slayers like the 7MM Rem Mag, .300 Win Mag, .300 Ultra Mag, or even a .338 Lapua can still run off, sometimes covering miles before piling up. As you may notice this is a rather limited list and is based upon purely upon my personal experience. While there are lesser legal calibers available that are clearly capable of killing elk, these lighter calibers with their lighter weight bullets put even greater performance constraints on the elk hunter. There can be any number of reasons for this, but the #1 reason for elk not dropping to the ground at the point of bullet impact is poor shot placement on the part of the elk hunter.

**Shot Placement**

Precise shot placement is essentially the result of six factors:
1. Effectively tuning the rifle, round, optics, and shooter
2. Practice
3. Familiarity with your setup
4. Practice
5. Practice
6. And finally you guessed it practice.

You can purchase the finest elk rifle available on the market, top it off with $2K-$3K optics with dial-in turrets, develop custom loads and still end up chasing your elk all over the mountain or worse missing the shot if you do not take the time to become "one with the rifle." There is no substitute for getting to know your weapon, its capabilities, quirks, and

179

limitations. I know a guy who went out and dropped a moderate $1,800 on his new elk rig and was "surprised" to learn from me that the factory load he was using would drop approximately 14 inches at 300 yards. His thinking was that this new round (lots of marketing publicity) and all the money he was spending might compensate for bullet drop and that bullet performance should be better because he had dropped a lot of cash. I guess it is better that he learned this at home rather than out in the field.

**Elk Hunter Tip: Know your weapon's operating characteristics and performance capabilities cold.**

If you plan on shooting factory loads as the majority of elk hunters do, I encourage you to get into the ballistic charts and look up the particular load/round, i.e. 150 grain Spitzer, 168 grain BTHP, 180 grain Swift Scirocco, etc. for your caliber rifle and find out what you can expect it to deliver at 100, 200, 300 yards and beyond. Then go to the range and validate this data with actual live fire. Keep in mind that you are looking for a caliber/load combination that will deliver a **minimum** of 1500 foot pounds of kinetic energy at the downrange point of impact.

In my early elk hunting days I hadn't learned how critical shooting with precision was. Considering the kill zone of an elk is approximately 18 inches in diameter, I figured that as long as my range shooting at 200 yards kept all the holes inside a pie plate or approximately 10 inches, I had plenty of room for error. Folks, this is a bunch of hogwash. When we are elk hunting, the target may move an inch or a foot this way or that between the time we tell our brain to pull the trigger and the time the bullet can travel down range to the target. In addition my experience has taught me, and maybe yours is different, there is rarely a

Jay Houston

bench, sandbags, and stool around to give me a rock steady shooting position when I am ready to take the shot in the field. It should not take a rocket scientist to see where this argument is going. In order to provide for the highest probability of making an accurate and straight away lethal shot, we need to take as many of the variables out of the shooting equation as possible. Factors such as weather, wind, moisture content in the air, altitude, your nerves, shooting position, availability or lack of a rest, and finally target angle and movement are just a few of the variables that come into play for each shot that you may encounter. It is our responsibility as ethical hunters to prepare ourselves to perform at our best.


## A Quick Word about Day Packs

Regardless of whether it's hanging on your back from your shoulders or riding over your backside and hanging from your waist, you will need some method for carrying your gear around in elk country. Personal preference will again prevail but here are some points to ponder as you consider which choice is right for you.

Backpacks or daypacks as they are sometimes called come in all sorts of sizes, colors, and configurations. Some have external frames, while others have internal frames or no frame at all. With the exception of those made particularly for hunting, most daypacks are made from some type of nylon material. In my opinion, this is not the best choice for elk hunting. Why? First, synthetics such as nylon are hard and noisy and will make all sorts of noise as you crawl through brush in elk country. Second most of these come in bright colors, which are fine for your middle schooler to take with him or her to class, but stand out like a sore thumb in elk country.

Jay Houston

A good elk hunting daypack should:
1) Be quiet
2) Be large enough to carry your essential gear for the day but no so large as to allow you the freedom to haul more gear than you need, 2500 cubic inches seems to be a good size
3) Be waterproof or at least water repellant, and finally
4) Have a support system that distributes the weight evenly between your shoulders and your hips. If the daypack that you are considering does not provide some type of waist/hip support, preferably padded, then you will be carrying the entire weight on your shoulders all day long. I can tell you from personal experience: this arrangement will wear you out in a hurry and may predispose you to leaving your gear back at camp the following day, which is neither a good nor a smart idea.

Another alternative is the fanny pack. This arrangement carries your gear in a pouch or series of pouches on your waist, usually just above your backside. For those of us with little to no backside, the fanny pack doesn't always stay where it is supposed to unless one cinches it up so tight as to cut off circulation to the lower half of the body. Some new models come with a set of shoulder straps to prevent this downward travel. Qualifications for a good fanny pack are the same as those for a good daypack.

Some hunting gear manufacturers have come out with a third alternative, a hybrid big game hunting vest/pack. These have pockets and pouches all over the place to stow your gear, much like those used by eastern turkey hunters. Using a vest type support system, my pack has numerous water repellant storage compartments, a compression storage area for holding a jacket, and a built in pouch and tube holder for a hydration system. This last feature is my favorite part as it allows me to carry 2 liters of water supported by the entire weight of the system. The tube allows me to have the water right at my fingertips. No more canteens trying to pull my pants down. No more water bottles sloshing around in a pocket. No more excess motion when I want a drink. Just bite the tube tip opening the valve, drink, and I'm done. Another added plus is that as the water is depleted in the bladder, it collapses taking less room and preventing the water from sloshing around making unwanted noise.

## Optics

I cannot tell you how many times I have heard the following statement with which I wholeheartedly agree, "Don't go cheap on optics." This means buy the very best optics that your budget will reasonably allow. So many times I've seen or heard of elk hunters who have dropped anywhere from $600 to $2,500 on a new elk rifle and then topped it off with a low end low quality scope.

If you have done any amount of research at all on rifle scopes you will have discovered that scope prices can vary anywhere from a basic (useless for elk hunting) $69.95 discount store special to $2,000 or more for higher end optics. Personally, I have always been a middle of the road buyer, but my personal budget leans to the lower end of that middle point. Over the years, I have discovered a number of manufacturers that produce what I consider to be reasonable quality optics that will fit within my personal budget limitations of $300 - $500. Manufacturers like Nikon, Vortex, Leupold, Bushnell, Alpen and Burris

183

all produce quality optics in this price range. If your pocketbook can stand it, Nightforce, Zeiss, Leica, and Swarovski produce excellent rifle optics as well, but be prepared to spend well upwards of $1500.

When you are shopping for your next riflescope a few attributes to consider are: Do you really need a variable power scope or will a fixed power such as a 4X or 6X suffice? While I use an adjustable 4-12X to help me identify my target at longer ranges (350-450 yards), there can be a downside to the use of variable power scopes. One problem is that you may forget to crank it back down from its higher magnification setting before attempting to take a close range shot. Additionally your field of view (lateral distance) will decrease significantly as you increase magnification. A case in point occurred during a guided elk hunt in New Mexico.

During the course of a day's hunt, the hunter had cranked his scope up to its maximum magnification for one reason or another and forgotten that he had left it on that setting despite numerous "reminders" not to do so by his guide. Later in the day, the hunter was fortunate enough to find himself in the position to take a shot at a nice bull. When the hunter, having traveled clear across the country for this hunt of a lifetime and full of "bull fever" attempted to place the cross hairs on the bull, you guessed it; all the hunter saw was brown hair. Fearing that he would lose this opportunity he fired. The result was...you guessed it again...a missed shot at what was later determined to be roughly 20 paces or about 60 yards. When the dust had settled, everyone was trying to figure out how he could have missed what should have been a slam dunk shot at such close range? A quick examination of the hunter's rifle answered the question. As suspected his variable power scope was again set to its maximum magnification. I wish I could have been there to see the look on the guide and hunters' faces. There are few things that will get a guide angry more than discovering that one of his hunters is not holding up their end of the bargain, especially after they have been warned on several occasions. I guess the lesson learned here is, unless you are using a fixed power scope; if you're adjusting the magnification feature, make sure that you return it to its lowest setting when you are done. I am religious about this, like locking the car in a parking lot.

**Elk Hunter Tip: Don't endanger another hunter by using your rifle optics to check out the area. Use a good set of binoculars or a spotting scope.**

A second feature that needs to be considered when looking for a new rifle scope is the eye relief distance for variable magnification scopes. I am not the guru on this. I just know from my own experience and that of others. When some variable power scopes are in the proper eye position for shooting and you adjust the magnification setting from say 3x to a higher magnification, you may have to readjust the position of your eye (or the scope) either towards or away from the rear of the scope to keep the entire field of view in sight. From a hunter's point of view this is really frustrating and under the right circumstances could cause a missed opportunity. Typically this problem can be avoided by purchasing better optics. A 3.5-4.0 inch eye relief works well for most.

A third factor to consider is the use of single piece tube construction for your scope. Better scopes are single piece tubes of either a 1 inch or 30mm diameter. It doesn't take a rocket scientist to figure out that the more pieces the tube is made of, the more the chance of something inside become misaligned. So stick with single piece tubes. Enough said.

Jay Houston

Finally, quality optics can significantly reduce the amount of eyestrain that the user will experience. I learned this lesson years ago from a long time firearm expert, ex-Army marksman and armorer. This same truth was recently confirmed just recently by a call I placed to a major optics manufacturer.

When the manufacturer of an optical lens begins to grind a lens, he starts grinding the lens at its center, grinding outward in an ever-larger circular pattern similar to the growth rings on a tree. In most cases, lower priced optics will only have their lenses ground out from the center a small portion of the actual radius of the lens. When one's eye attempts to focus through this partially ground lens, the eye will try to focus not only on the clear ground area but on the opaque unground area as well, which can produce eye strain. As a rule, higher quality lenses have a higher proportion of the lens ground out to 100%, thus providing the viewer with a much clearer image and reducing the likelihood of eyestrain.

Try this test for yourself. Go to your local sporting goods optics distributor. The test works best with binoculars, as they are easier to view for a period of time. Ask the sales clerk to escort you outside with two pairs of binoculars, one in the $100.00 range and the other in the $350.00 - $500.00 range. Try each pair out by holding it to your eyes for a minimum of one minute like you were glassing a far away hillside for elk. Now try the other pair, same deal. OK, compare the two as they pertain to the strain on your eyes. I've done this exercise many times and in every case, the higher quality set of optics wins out hands down when it comes to the amount of eyestrain experienced.
**Elk Hunter Tip: Don't go cheap on optics.**

# Selecting a Really Good Outfitter, The Right Stuff

Most of my guided elk hunts have been with outstanding outfitters and guides; unfortunately, I have unwittingly hunted with and know of a few real boneheads that have no sensible justification for calling themselves an outfitter. So what constitutes the right stuff when it comes to a quality outfitter or guide? Perhaps we first need to clarify the difference between the role of an outfitter and that of a guide.

For purposes of this discussion I am going to refer to the **Outfitter** as the individual that owns and manages the business. In many cases however, the outfitter/owner also acts as a guide as the need arises.  He or she is the one you will talk to when you call inquiring about a hunt. The outfitter's name is on the corporate documents; he or she pays for the insurance policy, and they may own all the camp gear as well as the stock used to haul hunters to and from camp. An outfitter typically fronts all the yearlong costs of operating and managing the company, including paying massive upfront lease payments to a landowner if the outfitter offers hunts on private land. Lease payments are out-of pocket expenses paid months or years in advance and can cost the outfitter $250,000 a year or more depending upon the size of the property and the history the property has for producing quality game.  He or she is often the face you see in the booth at outdoor and hunting shows across the country. Theirs is also the name that you will see on the contract that you sign for your future hunt. Bottom line, the outfitter is the person responsible for just about everything provided during the course of your hunt.

A **Guide** is usually an employee of the outfitter engaged to accompany the hunter in the field throughout his hunt. A good guide will have practical experience and a solid working knowledge of the land, the game, and managing people, specifically hunters. Your guide will roll out of his or her bedroll 1-2 hours before your alarm goes off and most nights will continue to work on your behalf long after you have returned to the warmth of your tent. Before you make a judgment call on the paycheck a guide receives, which really isn't a lot, remember to do the math and calculate the number of actual hours that guide has dedicated to you, your comfort, your safety and the successful outcome of your hunt. Folks, most guides don't do it for the money. They choose to be guides because they love to hunt; they love the work and the country that they get to work in. I have never met a guide that didn't enjoy the success of their hunter. It's your guide's job to be able to evaluate a hunter's ability to handle the long treks required every day in elk country, and to know just how far they can push the hunter towards his or her goal before giving them a rest break.

Last time I checked there were about 900 outfitters in my home state of Colorado that were registered with the State of Colorado Department of Regulatory Agencies (source: DORA). To the best of my knowledge, there are no official records of non-registered outfitters, however reliable sources suggest that there may as many as 300 individuals acting or marketing themselves as an outfitter in Colorado alone. These folks have no state registration, probably have no insurance, may have no first-aid training, and may have no experience whatsoever acting in the legal capacity of an outfitter. Believe it or not, I have personally talked with people who wanted me to broker hunts for them who considered themselves outfitters based upon one criteria, they either owned or managed a piece of property. Never going to happen folks!

Let's take a quick look at what constitutes a quality outfitter. Here are six attributes that I believe must be evident to constitute a good outfitter.

1. Integrity
2. Knowledge of land, elk, hunting strategies, and people
3. Experience on the ground with real people hunting real elk
4. Registered with the state regulatory agency for outfitters
5. Verifiable references
6. Quality Guides and Gear

Integrity: Integrity means that an outfitter and all those who work for him or her are people in whom you can place your trust. They are straight shooters who are going to tell you God's absolute truth whether you want to hear it or not. They will only promise to deliver that which they can reasonably expect to deliver. They do not "stretch" a story to make it more appealing ...except maybe around the fire after a long days hunt. They will back up whatever they say with action and are not afraid to be held accountable for their promises or other statements. They respect the land and their actions are always within the law and regulations of the regulatory agencies appointed over them and the land that they are licensed to use. Registered outfitters are required (in Colorado) to provide you with a contract of services. The language in this contract is stipulated by the regulatory agency and gives a clear definition of those services that the outfitter is going to provide and what you as a hunter can reasonable expect in return for your check.

Knowledge: A good outfitter or guide will have a thorough working understanding of: 1) The land whether it be private land, National Forest, or BLM land, 2) The elk...their travel patterns, feeding and bedding areas, and their escape routes when pressured in a particular area, 3) A broad variety of hunting techniques including spot and stalk, still hunting, and stand hunting, 4) People skills...this is critical as the last thing you need is some outfitter or guide chewing your backside off because he doesn't like you, 5) Camp management, 6) Business practices, and 7) The abilities of his guides and his stock just to round out the list. Here is a quick perspective on the people skills issue. I recently heard the story of an outfitter who is reputed to have fired a gun at the feet of one of his hunters (like in the movies) because the hunter said something the outfitter didn't like. Now I cannot verify the truth of this, but it did come from a fairly reliable source. These are the guys that give legitimate outfitters a bad name and, in my opinion, might need to spend some time in a very small room as a guest of the government for a while.

Experience:  All the book knowledge in the world cannot make one a good outfitter or guide if the knowledge has yet to be taken to the field and tested and refined on the land. Books are great, but experience is the true measure of what works and what doesn't in a particular situation.

Registered: The difference between a registered and an unregistered outfitter boils down to one issue, accountability. The registered outfitter recognizes his or her responsibilities and duties to the hunter, the state, and the public in general, and is willing for someone else to hold them accountable. The unlicensed outfitter (where it is required) is essentially an outlaw and doesn't really care about any of the above. He or she is only interested in his or her own welfare. These individuals have little regard for the law, the public, or the hunter. Steer clear. If a deal sounds too good to be true...it probably is.

Verifiable References: If an outfitter is reputable, he or she will be more than willing to grant ready access to references of both good and bad hunting experiences. In addition, in the state of Colorado, DORA (Department of Regulatory Agencies) maintains an online database of complaints and sanctions against any registered outfitter as well as actions taken.

Quality Gear and Guides: A good outfitter doesn't go cheap. He delivers a quality hunting experience for a fair and competitive price, and does not make excuses. His accommodations, sleeping arrangements, stock, tack, and camp equipment are serviceable, healthy, and in good repair. His guides know the land, the elk, their travel habits, their feeding and bedding locations, and where their water sources are. They are in good physical shape capable of hunting from dawn till dark. If hunting from horses or mules, they are well trained in the management and handling of the animals and know how to minimize the risk of an accident for themselves and their hunters. They have excellent people skills and know when and how to tell a hunter "no." As hunters, we must realize that it is not only the guide's responsibility to provide us with the best hunting experience that he can, but he is also responsible for our welfare and safety. If that means that he needs to draw the line to keep us safe, then he needs to have the skills to do that.

If you are considering an outfitter or guide and are concerned about how to go about picking a good one, run them up against the list above.

191

Jay Houston

Do all the research on the one that you like the best, and then ask yourself if the deal seems reasonable. If it sounds too good to be true, it probably is and maybe you best keep on looking.

SPECIAL NOTE ON PRICING: The available supply of quality guided or private land elk hunts in any given year is relatively limited when compared to the massive numbers of hunters seeking one of these hunts. Just like any other product or service there is a range of prices for these hunts. Learn the range and avoid hunts offered outside of the range. If the hunt is priced below the market's range, there is probably a good reason...they are worthless, otherwise the outfitter could price them within the market range. I urge you to avoid cheapo guided or private land hunts at all cost. They are just not worth the hassle. If the price is outside of the range on the high end, you need to discover the answer to the question...why? Generally the price of one of these higher end guided or private land hunts is due to one of two reasons: 1) The outfitter consistently exceeds the expectations of his clients delivering trophy class bulls or 2) The owner of the leased hunting property is charging the outfitter a premium lease price...probably due to reason #1. Either way, if you hope to hunt private land and/or true trophy class bulls, you can expect to pay premium prices.

Dickering for price in this business is in my opinion disrespectful of the outfitter. For any given hunt, regardless of the out of pocket price to the hunter, after all expenses are paid, the outfitter may show a $500 profit which really is not much given the outfitters out of pocket investment. I believe everyone deserves reasonable compensation and when a perspective hunter wants to dig into what works out to less than $100 per day to save a buck... well that is in my opinion, selfish. Your outfitter works extremely hard 365 days a year to maintain and promote the business that you will only experience for five days. Most such elk hunts are well worth the full price of the hunt.

Most western states have a regulatory agency responsible for the licensing of big game outfitters and or guides. If you are doing your due diligence checking out an outfitter for a future hunt, I strongly encourage you to contact the regulatory agency in that state in the early stages of the process to get a look at their record. Look for a current license, and few if any infractions. If you find an outfitter whose license has been revoked in the past...walk away! Outfitters with negative remarks or activities are just not worth your trouble. In most cases this information is available online. If the information is not available online, give them a call. The following is a list of these agencies and links to their website (effective 2016):

Colorado Department of Regulatory Agencies
https://www.colorado.gov/dora/licensing/Lookup/LicenseLookup.aspx

New Mexico Game and Fish Department
http://www.wildlife.state.nm.us/hunting/guide-outfitter-information/

Montana Department of Labor and Industry
https://ebiz.mt.gov/pol/

Wyoming Board of Outfitters
http://outfitters.state.wy.us/index.aspx

Idaho Outfitters and Guides Licensing Board
https://oglb.idaho.gov/

Oregon State Marine Board
https://www.oregon.gov/OSMB/Pages/Guides-Charters.aspx

Utah Division of Occupational and Professional licensing
https://secure.utah.gov/llv/search/search.html

Nevada Department of Wildlife
http://www.ndow.org/Forms_and_Resources/Licensed_Guides_Taxidermists_and_Other_Services/

Arizona
The state of Arizona does not offer or require an "Outfitter" license. Outfitters are generally defined in many jurisdictions as an enterprise that provides equipment or supplies, or a commercial pack or camp service, other than assisting for pay in the taking of wildlife.
https://www.azgfd.com/Hunting/Guides

# Wrapping it Up

If you have made it this far, you have heard terms like grit, commitment, effort, perseverance, planning, and knowledge over and over. These are your Silver Bullets. Insert these into your chamber, lock and load. Make these the cornerstones of every elk hunt from this day forward and you will triple your chances of success.

**Hic Sunt Dracones**
In ancient times those who traveled to far off places navigated by the position of the sun during the day and the stars and planets at night using charts (maps) that were drawn using the knowledge of those who had traveled before them. Mapmakers skilled in cartography hand drew the charts to include all the detail available at the time. When they came to an area for which there was no known reported data they wrote upon their maps, *Hic Sunt Dracones*, Latin for [Beyond] Here Be Dragons meaning dangerous or unexplored territories.

Successful elk hunters not only stay at it longer, they are willing to go farther. They are willing to venture into that unexplored territory…*hic sunt dracones*. They are prepared mentally and physically to move across one drainage into the next, and the next, and the next if that is what it takes. Elk are where we find them, which is rarely where we want them to be.

Jay Houston

I met a man once who ran marathons. I am not a runner, never have been and never want to be. Twenty-six grueling miles is far beyond anything I want to try but this guy was driven, devoted, committed...prepared. But that is not the real nugget. If called upon by a buddy at the end of such a body breaking race, he would turn around and run it all over again without missing a step. I don't really understand what possessed this soldier to do this, but I admire him. At perhaps some lesser level, this inner drive (Grit) is what pushes successful elk hunters to keep going over the next mountain. These are the elk hunters that consistently leave elk camp with full coolers.

I want to again acknowledge those folks who contributed their own knowledge and experience to this volume: Roger Medley, Bill Carmen, Paige Darden (My Topo team), and John L. Plaster. My enduring thanks to you all.

Remember what I said at the beginning:

*If you apply the information I have shared with you consistently you can increase your chances of success from the average 8-12 percent to the 40 percent range of the most successful elk hunters.*

God willing maybe we will share a campfire someday. Now, get out there and get at it.

Now say this out loud:

### KNOWLEDGE + EFFORT+ PERSERVERENCE=

### MY ELK HUNTING SILVER BULLET

Jay Houston

If you have questions about elk hunting or are considering booking your next big game hunt, I can be reached at:

Email: jay@huntconnections.com

**Check out my online resources at:**

www.elkcamp.com
www.huntconnections.com
www.jay-houston.com

Jay Houston

## Image Credits

Roger Medley: Front Cover Bull Elk, Bull Page 8, Herd page 68, page 131, page 157.

Kevin Fair: Makenna's bull page 46, Jay's bull page 53, Kevin's bull page 120

Rob Springer (Hunter): Page 53

Bill Carmen (Hunter): Page 57

Steve Rinella (Hunter): Page 161

Jerry Gowins (Photographer): Page 93

Jason Balaz (Hunter): Page 110

Barnett Crossbows (Product): Page 146

Cover background image courtesy of Kryptek Outdoor Group

RMEF logo image courtesy of Rocky Mountain Elk Foundation

Images of author taken by Rae Ann Houston

Hunt Connections graphic courtesy of Jackson Creek Media Group, Inc.

**A 100% <u>Personalized</u> Elk Hunting Experience**

Whether you're hunting the Colorado high country, the sage flats of New Mexico or Utah, or the steep slopes of Idaho or western Montana; hunting the back country where few hunters tread with a professional and knowledgeable guide is the pinnacle of the big game hunting experience.

## What Sets Hunt Connections Apart

**A Personalized Hunting Experience**

If you want an elk hunt built around your individual requirements, we are the guys. Since 1996 we have provided every one of our hunters with a <u>100% personalized hunting experience</u> tailored precisely to their individual requirements, physical ability, and financial situation.

It doesn't cost any more...**it's just a better hunting experience**.

**Contact us at : Jay Houston, <u>jay@huntconnections.com</u>,**
**888.360.HUNT**

199

www.ingramcontent.com/pod-product-compliance
Lightning Source LLC
Chambersburg PA
CBHW052000090426
42741CB00008B/1479